Cambridge Elements ≡

Elements in Quantitative and Computational Methods for the
Social Sciences
edited by
R. Michael Alvarez
California Institute of Technology
Nathaniel Beck
New York University

ADAPTIVE INVENTORIES

A Practical Guide for Applied Researchers

Jacob M. Montgomery
Washington University in St. Louis

Erin L. Rossiter
University of Notre Dame

CAMBRIDGE
UNIVERSITY PRESS

CAMBRIDGE
UNIVERSITY PRESS

University Printing House, Cambridge CB2 8BS, United Kingdom

One Liberty Plaza, 20th Floor, New York, NY 10006, USA

477 Williamstown Road, Port Melbourne, VIC 3207, Australia

314–321, 3rd Floor, Plot 3, Splendor Forum, Jasola District Centre,
New Delhi – 110025, India

103 Penang Road, #05–06/07, Visioncrest Commercial, Singapore 238467

Cambridge University Press is part of the University of Cambridge.

It furthers the University's mission by disseminating knowledge in the pursuit of
education, learning, and research at the highest international levels of excellence.

www.cambridge.org
Information on this title: www.cambridge.org/9781108797269
DOI: 10.1017/9781108862516

First published 2022

A catalogue record for this publication is available from the British Library.

ISBN 978-1-108-79726-9 Paperback
ISSN 2398-4023 (online)
ISSN 2514-3794 (print)

Additional resources for this publication at www.cambridge.org/adaptiveinventories

Adaptive Inventories

A Practical Guide for Applied Researchers

Elements in Quantitative and Computational Methods for the Social Sciences

DOI: 10.1017/9781108862516
First published online: July 2022

Jacob M. Montgomery
Washington University in St. Louis

Erin L. Rossiter
University of Notre Dame

Author for correspondence: Jacob M. Montgomery,
jacob.montgomery@wustl.edu

Abstract: The goal of this Element is to provide a detailed introduction to adaptive inventories, an approach to making surveys adjust to respondents' answers dynamically. This method can help survey researchers measure important latent traits or attitudes accurately while minimizing the number of questions respondents must answer. The Element provides both a theoretical overview of the method and a suite of tools and tricks for integrating it into the normal survey process. It also provides practical advice and direction on how to calibrate, evaluate, and field adaptive batteries using example batteries that measure a variety of latent traits of interest to survey researchers across the social sciences.

Keywords: survey methods, computerized adaptive testing, latent variable, active learning, measurement

ISBNs: 9781108797269 (PB), 9781108862516 (OC)
ISSNs: 2398-4023 (online), 2514-3794 (print)

Contents

1 Introducing Adaptive Inventories

Technology has revolutionized how social scientists administer surveys, recruit participants, and design survey instruments. Even 20 years ago, collecting survey data was an onerous and expensive task requiring either the assistance of professional firms or hours of work by expansive research teams. Today, easy-to-use survey administration software can be paired with readily available pools of online respondents to implement and field a survey in a matter of hours.

However, in many ways, little has changed. Most surveys are entirely static. And to the extent surveys vary from person to person, the survey adapts not in *response* to inputs, but rather the instrument is pre-programmed (e.g., randomization). The textbook process remains that questions are written, evaluated, and placed on surveys. Once the instrument is designed, however, it changes little based on the input from respondents.

This is not to say that researchers have not innovated. Salganik and Levy (2015), for instance, propose a wiki survey battery where respondents can alter response options. Groves and Heeringa (2006) propose an influential responsive sampling framework where survey *mode* adapts systemically to optimize response rates while controlling costs. Moore and Moore (2013) propose a method for dynamic assignment in sequential experiments to maximize balance. However, none of these approaches is adaptive in the sense of active learning, where the goal is to alter the content of the survey interactively to maximize learning about some quantity of interest. Conceptually, the most similar work to our own is Offer-Westort, Coppock, and Green (2019), who apply a bandit approach to adapt treatment assignment propensities.

This is unfortunate for two reasons. First, the use of online surveys makes it possible to rethink how surveys work so they are responsive, less burdensome, and better suited to researcher needs. After all, wouldn't it be better if surveys could "think for themselves" a bit and adapt as the interview proceeds? Second, the active learning framework has been widely applied in computer science, engineering, and more. This research shows that algorithms designed to optimize data collection can dramatically improve estimates and reduce overhead in terms of time or money (see, e.g., Miller, Linder, and Mebane (2019) and Enamorado (2018) for recent examples).

The goal of this Element is to provide a detailed introduction to one such approach for making surveys "smarter." Specifically, we introduce adaptive inventories (AIs), a method that can help survey researchers measure important latent traits or attitudes accurately while minimizing the number of questions respondents answer.

In the following sections, we provide both a theoretical overview of the method and a suite of tools and tricks for integrating AIs into the survey process. But first, let's clarify the "problem" that needs solving. What exactly is wrong with traditional batteries?

1.1 Motivating Example: Measuring Political Knowledge

Imagine a researcher wants to measure respondents' levels of political knowledge. Tasks like this are common but actually represent a thorny problem. To begin, the concept of interest is latent, we cannot assess it directly. A respondent's "knowledge" is too abstract to be measured using one single question. Knowledge is not like, say, one's vote choice that respondents can plausibly report directly.

When measuring latent constructs, scholars must instead rely on survey items that relate to the concept indirectly and imperfectly. The consequence is that in order to measure the concept accurately, researchers need to ask each respondent multiple questions and aggregate their responses. Indeed, roughly speaking, the more questions we ask, the better our final measure will be. Following this logic, there is always an incentive to ask more questions about important latent constructs.

In the specific case of political knowledge, these items might ask about important political leaders, the rules of the constitutional system, and the basic contours of political debates and party competition. For example, Figure 1 shows questions adapted from the 1991 American National Election Study (ANES) Pilot, which included 20 political knowledge questions.

However, there are clear costs to batteries like this. In most situations, lengthy batteries are too expensive to administer as they take up too much valuable survey space. Moreover, answering long (and often repetitive) survey batteries is tedious for respondents. Attrition can increase (e.g., Sheatsley 1983) and answers become less informative (e.g., Herzog and Bachman 1981).

Faced with this dilemma, the standard approach for measuring concepts like political knowledge is as follows:

- First, administer a large set of items to a sample of respondents.
- Second, use this pilot data to evaluate the items and select *one subset* to include on the survey. (This second step is typically done with some measurement model, such as factor analysis.)

In the case of the political knowledge battery, this standard procedure was followed almost exactly. Using the ANES pilot data, Delli Carpini and Keeter

1. **Do you happen to know what job or political office is now held by Kamala Harris?**

2. Do you happen to know what job or political office is now held by Chuck Schumer?

3. Do you happen to know what job or political office is now held by John Roberts?

4. Do you happen to know what job or political office is now held by Vladimir Putin?

5. Do you happen to know what job or political office is now held by Boris Johnson?

6. Do you happen to know what job or political office is now held by Nancy Pelosi?

7. Do you happen to know how many times an individual can be elected President?

8. How long is the term of office for a United States Senator?

9. **How much of a majority is required for the US Senate and House to override a Presidential veto?**

10. What are the first ten amendments to the US Constitution called?

11. **Whose responsibility is it to decide if a law is constitutional or not? Is it the President, the Congress, or the Supreme Court?**

12. Whose responsibility is it to nominate judges to the Federal Courts? Is it the President, the Congress, or the Supreme Court?

13. Which of the two major parties is considered to be more conservative?

14. Do you happen to know which party has the most members in the House of Representatives in Washington?

15. **Do you happen to know which party has the most members in the US Senate?**

16. **Would you say that one of the parties is more conservative than the other at the national level? Which party is more conservative?**

17. Would you say that one of the parties supports increasing defense spending more than the other at the national level? Which party most supports increasing defense spending?

18. Would you say that one of the parties is supports increasing defense spending more than the other at the national level? Which party most supports increasing defense spending?

19. Would you say that one of the parties supports having the government provide more services at the national level? Which party most supports the government providing many more services?

20. Would you say that one of the parties supports having the government make every effort to improve the social and economic position of blacks? Which party most supports the government making every effort to improve the social and economic position of blacks?

Figure 1 Items measuring political knowledge (bold items selected for reduced measure)

chose the five items bolded in Figure 1. These became a canonical measure of political knowledge (Delli Carpini and Keeter 1993, 1996).

So, what's the problem? In reducing these larger batteries down to a manageable size, the traditional strategy requires researchers to choose a *single* subset of items to administer to *everyone*. That is, the most knowledgeable and the least knowledgeable respondents will answer the exact same set of questions. This strategy is inefficient. When we administer the same static battery to the entire sample, it inevitably includes some items that provide little additional information about specific respondents' true latent positions.

To make this clearer, consider Question 2 (Q2) asking respondents to identify Chuck Schumer as the Majority Leader of the US Senate. Would this be a good question to add to the canonical five-item battery? The answer is, *it depends on a respondent's answers to the other items*. For some respondents, their answer to this question would be useful. When interviewing a respondent who has already answered five other questions correctly, Q2 might represent a good test to distinguish the modestly knowledgeable from the most knowledgeable. We know that the respondent is fairly knowledgeable, but we are not sure if she can recognize more obscure political figures. In other words, based on what we know so far, she could plausibly get the question right or wrong, and we will learn something from her answer.

But imagine a respondent who has failed to identify the Vice President and cannot identify the Republican Party as being conservative. Based on what we already know, asking him about Schumer serves little purpose. The respondent will almost surely answer incorrectly. Thus, when he gets it wrong (exactly what we expected based on his previous responses), we do not really learn anything. But what if we adjust the battery based on the respondents' previous answers? Then, we could ask a question designed to distinguish the somewhat unknowledgeable from the completely ignorant, and our estimates will be more precise.

These examples illustrate the root problem with the traditional approach. By choosing the same set of questions to administer to *all* respondents, researchers are neglecting valuable information that they have already collected. Namely, they are ignoring previous responses to questions in the battery. Instead, we should use what we learn from previous responses to *customize* batteries to each respondent. And by asking better, more informative questions, we will improve our final measure.

1.2 AIs and Computerized Adaptive Testing

The goal of AIs is to tailor the battery for each respondent based on what is learned during the course of the survey. Rather than ask the full battery or fixed subset of questions, an algorithm picks the next question for each respondent. This amounts to an alternative procedure for developing surveys:

- First, administer a large set of items to a sample of respondents.
- Second, allow *an algorithm* to use this pilot data to select a subset of questions *for each respondent*.

When implemented correctly, the resulting latent trait estimates will be less biased, more precise (lower variance), and more efficient. Moreover, the adaptive battery takes up no additional survey time. Better measurement; same low cost!

To achieve this goal, we draw on the rich literature on computerized adaptive testing (CAT), which was originally developed in the field of educational testing (e.g., Kingsbury and Weiss 1983; Weiss 1982; Weiss and Kingsbury

1984). You are most likely to see CAT applied to educational testing programs (e.g., the Graduate Management Admissions Test), physical and mental health assessments (e.g., the National Institutes of Health Patient-Reported Outcomes Measurement Information System), or employee selection and placement (e.g., the Armed Services Vocational Aptitude Test Battery). Indeed, many readers may be intimately familiar with CAT methods as they have been used on the Graduate Record Exam (GRE).

1.3 A Brief Introduction to CAT

Figure 2 illustrates the basics of a CAT algorithm. Each of the four circles corresponds to a step in the procedure. These steps are as follows: estimate a respondent's position on the latent trait of interest; select the next item to administer that optimizes some objective function; administer that item and record the response; check the stopping rule(s) and either continue questioning or return the final estimate of the respondent's position (Segall 2005).

CAT needs two sources of information to complete the procedure: properties of the question items and respondents' answers as they advance through the survey. To explain, let's return to the researcher wishing to measure political knowledge. First, she needs information about the question items, such as how "difficult" the questions are. She gathers this information by pretesting

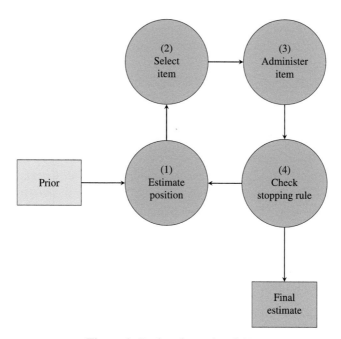

Figure 2 Basic schematic of AIs

the battery with a calibration sample. That is, she must give the *full battery* of question items to some sample to understand which survey items are easier or harder and also which items are more reliable indicators of political knowledge. While the full battery needs to be evaluated to generate these item-level parameters, it is possible to do this effectively without giving the full battery to everyone with split sample designs.

Second, the researcher needs to generate guesses about the respondents' levels of political knowledge as they take the survey. For this, the algorithm simply needs the respondents' answers to questions in the battery so far.

Taking these pieces of information together, CAT tailors which questions are administered to each respondent. For a respondent who has already identified Nancy Pelosi (Q6 in Figure 1), it is not useful to ask her to identify Kamala Harris (Q1). Rather, the algorithm will ask the respondent to identify the Bill of Rights (Q10). How does it know to do this? CAT uses item-level information – Q1 is relatively easy and Q10 is relatively hard. Next, CAT will use the fact that the respondent answered Q6 correctly to inform our beliefs about her level of knowledge (that it is high). Combining our beliefs about the respondent and our beliefs about these questions, we can then reasonably infer that asking Q10 will be more informative than asking Q1.

1.4 Example: An Adaptive Measure of Political Knowledge

Of course, AIs are easier to describe than to implement. Intuitively, they are attractive because there are no additional costs in terms of survey time. But there are still a number of logistical hurdles to overcome and assumptions we must satisfy. How would this work in practice? Answering this question will be one of the primary goals of this Element. However, as a first pass, we provide a simple example focused again on measuring political knowledge.

This example will use the catSurv software, an open-source R package that we designed specifically for the needs of survey researchers (Montgomery and Rossiter 2017). This Element will provide detailed examples using catSurv to facilitate understanding of the CAT algorithm and how researchers might implement AIs in their own work. In addition to this Element, we provide extensive help files with examples in the package documentation at https://cran.r-project.org/web/packages/catSurv/catSurv.pdf.[1]

To follow along with the code using R or RStudio on your machine, you need to install and load the package using the following two lines:

---

[1] Users who wish to compile their own version of the package will need to take additional steps to configure their machine to correctly handle the C++ code contained in catSurv. Visit https://catsurv.com for additional details.

```
install.packages("catSurv")
library(catSurv)
```

Alternatively, all code used throughout the Element is stored in a Code Ocean Capsule and can be executed online at `https://codeocean.com/capsule/2685679/tree`.

1.4.1 Setting Up an Adaptive Inventory

The first step is to write a set of question items that could potentially be administered to respondents. In this case, we will use the knowledge battery described by Montgomery and Cutler (2013). This consists of 64 multiple choice questions on topics similar to those in Figure 1.

The second step is to administer these questions to a calibration sample. We administered these items to a sample of about 800 respondents recruited from Amazon's Mechanical Turk service in 2012. This dataset codes answers as either correct (a value of "1") or incorrect ("0"). The data is included in the catSurv package and can be accessed using the following command.

```
data("polknowMT")
```

You can also view the help file for this dataset, or for any data or function in the package, by using the ? function, (for instance, ?polknowMT). This help file includes question wordings and response options.

With sample data in hand for the *full* battery, the next step is to calibrate the question item parameters using the `ltmCat()` function. This function creates an object of the class Cat. You may get a message that the measurement model is poorly estimated. This is largely a result of the quite small sample size used in this example. Section 6 provides additional guidance on appropriate sample sizes for calibration samples.

```
knowledgeCat <- ltmCat(polknowMT)
```

The `Cat-class` help file describes all of the elements of a Cat object. Importantly, a Cat object holds all the information about the question items needed for the battery to work. For instance, it contains the item parameters that indicate the difficulty of each question. You can see the first six difficulty parameters with the @ symbol.

```
head(knowledgeCat@difficulty)
```

```
##        Q1       Q2       Q3       Q4       Q5       Q6
## 4.697249 3.887995 5.889785 1.191926 3.946480 2.535870
```

The design of `catSurv` means that all of the CAT options are chosen up front when you design the AI. For instance, we can indicate that our adaptive battery should only include two questions by setting the `LengthThreshold` slot. To do this, you alter the `CAT` object itself rather than including it as an argument when doing item selection.

```
setLengthThreshold(knowledgeCat)<-2
```

While this makes the initial setup more complex, actual administration of an AI requires little coding. Kaufman (2020), for instance, was able to incorporate an AI into an RShiny survey using only three lines of code.

1.4.2 AIs in Action

Now that the inventory is set up, choosing the next item to ask to a respondent is simple and fast using the `selectItem()` function.

```
selectItem(knowledgeCat)$next_item
```

```
## [1] 41
```

This function estimates the position of the respondent on the latent trait and chooses the optimal question to ask next. In this case, it indicates that item 41 should be asked.

As shown in Figure 2, the next step is to administer the question and record the response. In this case, we will imagine that the respondent answers question 41 correctly.

```
knowledgeCat<-storeAnswer(catObj=knowledgeCat, item=41, answer=1)
```

The next step is to check whether the stopping criteria was met. In this case, we specified that we only wish to ask two questions.

```
checkStopRules(knowledgeCat)
```

```
## [1] FALSE
```

Since the stopping point has not been reached (`checkStopRules()` returned a FALSE), the process repeats.

```
selectItem(knowledgeCat)$next_item
```

```
## [1] 49
```

```
knowledgeCat<-storeAnswer(catObj=knowledgeCat, item=49, answer=0)
checkStopRules(knowledgeCat)
```

```
## [1] TRUE
```

After administering a second item and storing the answer, the stopping rule has now been reached and the AI is finished. The final step is simply to estimate the respondent's position on the latent trait.

```
estimateTheta(catObj=knowledgeCat)
```

```
## [1] 0.0627642
```

This is the final estimate for this respondent's score on the political knowledge scale.

While AIs using `catSurv` require some work, the actual implementation requires only four functions: `selectItem`, `storeAnswer`, `checkStopRules`, and `estimateTheta`. And, as shown in Montgomery and Cutler (2013), AIs of political knowledge provide significantly improved estimates of the latent trait relative to fixed batteries of the same length.

1.5 Example Applications

Yes, AIs require extra work. Is it worth the trouble? Will implementing this technique actually change our substantive findings or help us to do better research? Our answer is that AIs offer a way to improve measurement of key latent variables, and this improved measurement can, in turn, improve our substantive findings. In essence, AIs can be used effectively whenever:

1. you want to measure a unidimensional[2] latent variable that will be an outcome, explanatory variable, or moderator;
2. you have space for at least three survey items for that trait;
3. the latent trait is associated with a large inventory where the number of potential items to include significantly exceeds the number of items you want to ask;
4. you are interested only in the underlying trait and not responses to individual items; and
5. you believe that the item calibration is stable from one sample to another.

These conditions apply in many settings across the social sciences whether one is trying to measure personality traits, ideology, cognitive skills, consumer sentiment, or other attributes. But some concrete examples will help set the stage. While the remainder of this Element focuses on mathematical foundations and practical considerations of AIs, we hope these examples serve as a

---

[2] As we discuss in Section 7, there are extensions to this framework that allow for multidimensional latent traits. However, all of the results in this Element assume a single underlying dimension.

backdrop to highlight that AIs can improve our ability to test theories and do better science. Our first example explicitly compares an adaptive and nonadaptive battery, while our second shows how AIs can be used on large national surveys. These examples are necessarily brief. For a fuller explanation of this data source and further results, see Montgomery and Rossiter (2020).

1.5.1 Adaptive Right-Wing Authoritarianism

The right-wing authoritarianism (RWA) trait captures individuals' differences regarding submission to authorities, tolerance of outgroups, and conventionalism (Altemeyer 1988). Political scientists have shown RWA explains reactions to ethno-racial diversity (Velez and Lavine 2017), the support of war (Hetherington and Suhay 2011), and even partisanship and increasing polarization (Hetherington and Weiler 2009).

While a widely used battery for measuring RWA has 30 items (Altemeyer 1988), the American National Election Pilot Study has asked a fixed subset of five of these items to reduce the inventory's length. To assess the implications of measuring RWA with an adaptive inventory, we conducted a study where we randomly assigned 1,335 participants to take either a *fixed* or *adaptive* five-item inventory. In either case, after answering five items, respondents completed the remaining battery items in a random order.

Figure 3 shows the distribution of latent trait estimates when measuring RWA using each of these five-item inventories (dashed lines) compared against RWA as estimated using the same respondents' full 30-item answer profiles (solid lines). When comparing the dashed and solid lines of each plot, we see that the adaptive inventory does a better job than the fixed inventory of estimating extreme positions on the latent scale, especially for low values of RWA.

Does that alter our inferences? To answer this, Figure 4 shows the difference in our understanding of how RWA relates to modern racism (Sidanius et al. 2004). Specifically, we estimated separate regressions using RWA estimates for respondents randomly assigned to the fixed inventories and the AIs.[3] Further, we used respondents' RWA estimates from their full response profiles to estimate "true" values of the RWA regression coefficients in each model. The lines in Figure 4 shows the regression coefficients (and 95 percent confidence intervals) estimated using RWA estimates from each five-item inventory and from the full 30-item inventory. In all, the censoring that results from using the fixed five-item inventory, shown in Figure 3, leads to an upward bias in the

---

[3] We control for race, gender, and level of education in each model. We used the same measurement model fit to a separate wave to estimate respondents' positions and ensure that all measures are on the same latent scale.

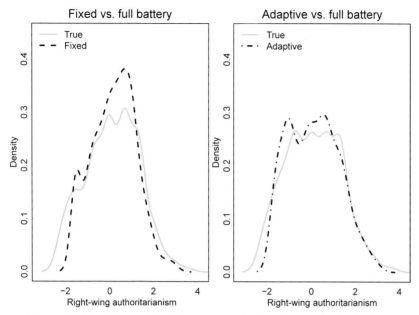

Figure 3 Adaptive and fixed measures of right-wing authoritarianism. Histograms of RWA as estimated using the fixed and adaptive five-item inventories (dashed lines) and the full 30-item inventory (solid lines)

coefficients. But, the coefficient estimates when using an adaptive five-item inventory and the full 30-item inventory barely differ.

1.5.2 Adaptive Need for Cognition

As a second example we turn to "need for cognition" (NFC). This trait, measuring "the tendency for an individual to engage in and enjoy thinking" (Cacioppo and Petty 1982, p. 116), is used often in political science and related fields. In particular, Druckman (2004) has shown that NFC is an important moderator for the effects of issue framing.

Here, we replicate this finding with a four-item adaptive NFC battery and a framing experiment, both included on the 2016 ANES Pilot Study conducted with YouGov. This example quickly illustrates how adaptive batteries can be implemented in social science surveys.

Specifically, the experiment asked participants to react to the following statement: "*There's been a lot of talk lately about political correctness. Some people think that the way people talk needs to change with the times to be more sensitive to people from different backgrounds. Others think that this has already gone too far and many people are just too easily offended. Which is closer to your opinion?*" (emphasis added).

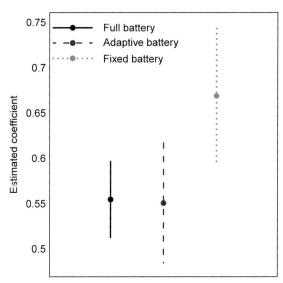

Figure 4 RWA regression coefficients comparing bias from adaptive and fixed inventories. Lines show RWA regression coefficients and 95 percent CIs from models explaining modern racism. The solid line is the coefficient and CI when using the full 30-item inventory, the dashed line is the coefficient and CI when using the five-item adaptive inventory, and the dotted line is the coefficient and CI when using the five-item fixed inventory.

Participants were randomly assigned to receive the statement with (n = 574) or without (n = 626) the first sentence framing the statement as a concern about political correctness. Response options ranged from 1 ("The way people talk needs to change a lot") to 4 ("People are much too easily offended"). We expect that this frame will have a positive effect among white respondents, but that it will be moderated by NFC.

Figure 5 shows the results of this interaction from weighted least squares regression using ANES weights.[4] The effect of the political correctness frame is modified by levels of NFC. For individuals at the high end of the trait, the framing had no statistically reliable effect. However, the frame has a significant effect for individuals at the low end of NFC, which is consistent with prior research (Druckman 2004).

1.6 Overview of the Element

This Element has two overarching goals. First, we hope to provide an approachable introduction to AIs. While many previous studies explain CAT algorithms

---

[4] We also controlled for ideology, party identification, education, gender, racial resentment, white racial identity, and a sense of white guilt.

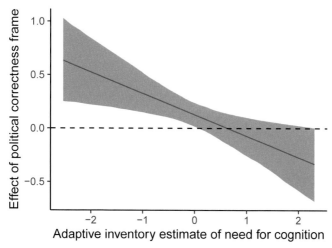

Figure 5 Interaction between NFC as measured by an adaptive battery and an experimental political correctness frame. Line represents framing effect across levels of NFC. Shaded region represents a 95 percent confidence interval. The experiment worked for individuals low on NFC, as we would expect from previous research.

see, e.g., Choi and Swartz (2009) and van der Linden and Pashley (2010) there is no canonical text that provides both a discussion of the method and examples of how it can be incorporated into surveys. Thus, the first goal of this Element is to introduce the intuition and mathematics behind AIs. We hope to show that despite some of the mathematical formalism, CAT algorithms are actually a very intuitive way to conduct dynamic item selection.

Our second goal is to provide practical solutions to some of the hurdles researchers will face. Specifically, we provide a suite of free tools intended to make integrating AIs into standard surveys as straightforward as possible. Throughout this Element, we will direct readers to these resources and provide examples and discussions.

The most important resource we discuss is the `catSurv` R package already mentioned. Using this software, we will provide examples of how AIs can be developed, fielded, and analyzed. We assume a basic level of familiarity with the R programming environment. We will primarily be using functions provided in either base R or the `catSurv` package. Where functions from other packages are used, we will use the package name directly in the function call. For instance, when using the `grm()` function (fitting a graded response model) in the `ltm` package, we write `ltm::grm()`. Users wishing to replicate our code will need to install these packages using the `install.packages()` command.

The other main tool we provide is `https://catsurv.com`, a cloud-based webservice that allows users to access `catSurv` functionality via application program interface (API) calls. This facilitates implementation of AIs into web-based services such as Qualtrics and can also be integrated by survey firms into their own platforms.

Finally, we provide pre-calibrated adaptive batteries for several prominent personality inventories including the big five (Costa and McCrae 2008), the Schwartz values index (Schwartz 1992), need for cognition (Cacioppo and Petty 1982), need to evaluate (Jarvis and Petty 1996), right-wing authoritarianism (Altemeyer 1988) and more. We calibrated these batteries with more than 1 million respondents from both nationally representative and convenience samples. This allows researchers to use adaptive methods without having to conduct their own pretest survey.

Organizationally, we begin simply. Section 2 provides a more grounded introduction to CAT methods using a detailed explanation of the default methods implemented in catSurv. This section gives readers a clearer understanding of the fundamental principles before muddying the waters with the alternatives. Section 3 provides a more thorough explanation of the various options for estimation routines, item selection criteria, and stopping rules available for inventories with binary outcomes. Section 4 then shows how the method can be extended to accommodate categorical responses.

At this point readers will have a wide array of potential choices. Section 5, therefore, turns to the question of how to decide which implementation is best and whether using CAT is worthwhile. In particular, we provide a set of diagnostic tools to let researchers compare and contrast performance using both real-world and simulated respondent data.

Section 6 then provides a more detailed discussion of practicalities. Exactly how can applied researchers incorporate an adaptive inventory into their own survey work? We provide recommendations and examples of how to collect and use calibration data and how AIs can actually be included on surveys. We conclude in Section 7 with a short discussion of CAT, its limitations, and future directions for continued research.

2 Introduction to CAT for Binary Outcomes

In this section, we walk through the basic steps of a standard CAT algorithm in detail. As we will discuss later, there are many ways to implement an AI. But to keep things simple, we will focus on just one here. This does not mean that this is the "best" algorithm, only that we felt that this particular set of choices was most useful for introducing the method. Once you have a stronger grasp of the basics, we will then be in a position to discuss different options in detail in Section 3.

Substantively, our focus in this section is the narcissistic personality inventory (NPI) (Raskin and Terry 1988). This is a widely used battery designed to measure respondents' "grandiose yet fragile sense of self and entitlement as well as a preoccupation with success and demands for admiration" (Ames, Rose, and Anderson 2006, pp. 440–441). However, this measure is largely missing from fields like political science that rely heavily on surveys. We suspect that this is at least partly a result of the length of the NPI instrument – it is 40 questions long! Computerized adaptive testing provides a way for researchers to include a reasonably sized NPI on future surveys.

We also use NPI because there are exactly two response options per item. Respondents are presented with two statements and asked to indicate which is most applicable to themselves. A simple example includes choosing: (A) "I have a natural talent for influencing people," or (B) "I am not good at influencing people." Having a binary outcome is helpful because the mathematical model underlying CAT algorithms, usually referred to as item response theory (IRT), differs when the question is binary or categorical. Although most survey batteries are categorical, the binary IRT model is easier to explain.

This section walks through the binary IRT model that underlies computerized adaptive testing and then details each step of the CAT algorithm.

- **Estimate position**: We use the **expected a posteriori** approach, which is just the expected value of the respondent's position on the latent trait.
- **Select item**: We use the **minimum expected posterior variance** criteria, which is designed to choose the item that will best reduce our uncertainty about the respondent in expectation.
- **Stopping rule**: We use the **length threshold** stopping rule that terminates the battery after a specific number of items has been asked.

2.1 Item Response Theory for Dichotomous Survey Responses

The NPI is an example of the simplest case for CAT since the respondent chooses between two options. Although this battery measures a personality trait, the discussion here applies to all cases with binary responses for a one-dimensional latent trait. Perhaps the response options are "yes" and "no," or perhaps it might be appropriate to classify responses as correct or incorrect (e.g., attention screeners (Berinsky et al. 2019)).

Before we can do anything adaptive, however, we first need a statistical model of our battery. We turn to this next, drawing extensively on the IRT models originating in educational testing.

2.1.1 Calculating Probabilities: The Item Response Function

To start, we need an item response function (IRF) for each question. The IRF is the conditional probability that a respondent provides a specific answer to a survey item given their position on the latent scale of interest. The IRF used in the catSurv package is shown in Equation 1. For respondent $j \in [1, J]$ and item $i \in [1, N]$, the probability that j answers with a '1' (answers the item correctly or chooses the second response option) is:

$$\Pr_i(y_{ij} = 1|\theta_j) = \frac{\exp(a_i + b_i\theta_j)}{1 + \exp(a_i + b_i\theta_j)}. \tag{1}$$

This is sometimes referred to as the two-parameter logistic (2PL) model.

In the binary setting, the probability that a respondent will answer with a '0' (answering the item incorrectly or choosing the first response option) is then $1 - \Pr_i(y_{ij} = 1|\theta_j)$. We use the $\Pr_i(\cdot)$ notation to emphasize that this function is defined differently for each item, although for expositional clarity we suppress dependence on the item-level parameters (a_i, b_i).

In this equation, θ_j is the respondent's position on the latent trait, a_i is item i's "difficulty parameter," and b_i is item i's "discrimination parameter." These English labels for the parameters derive from the educational testing literature and can be a bit confusing in a survey setting. But we stick with this canonical terminology since it is so widely used.

This discussion of a_i and b_i may seem a bit odd since the real goal is to learn about the latent position for a respondent, θ_j. But to do that we *first* need to estimate these item parameters. Recall, the idea behind CAT is that the algorithm determines which item will be most revealing for a specific respondent. These parameters, which determine the shape of the IRF, allow the algorithm to reason about items.

So where do the item parameters come from? We estimate these parameters using a *calibration sample* of responses to the full inventory. As an example, we use data from a convenience sample of respondents recruited via Amazon's Mechanical Turk who completed the 40-item NPI battery (see the help file in R using the command ?npi for additional information). For this example, we only use the first 500 respondents from this dataset so that the model fits quickly. As we discuss in Section 6, calibrations will usually require larger samples.

The ltmCat() function utilizes a marginal maximum likelihood algorithm provided in the ltm package (Rizopoulos 2006) to fit these models and set up a Cat object. The ltmCat() function also allows users to pass in models fit directly in the ltm::ltm() function. If you experience issues with the estimation (e.g., poor convergence), we recommend that you fit the model first using the 'ltm' package and pass the results into the ltmCat function. Further, you can also set these parameters manually from some other source using the `setDifficulty()` and `setDiscrimination()` functions.

```
data(npi) # load the NPI dataset
calibration_sample <- npi[1:500, ] # Use only the first 500 respondents
npi_cat <- ltmCat(calibration_sample) # Fit the model
```

The difficulty and discrimination parameters are now contained in the `Cat` object. You can access these parameters for the first question item using:

```
npi_cat@difficulty[1]
```

```
##            Q1
## -0.4880876
```

```
npi_cat@discrimination[1]
```

```
##           Q1
## 0.9750334
```

Now that we have the item parameters, we examine the shape of any IRF. One way to do this is just to calculate the height of this probability curve for different values of θ. The `catSurv` function `probability` will actually calculate the height of the IRF directly. The function takes as arguments an item and a specific location on the latent dimension, θ_j, for which we'd like to know the probability of a correct ('1') response. As with nearly all of `catSurv` functions, we must also specify the `Cat` object of interest.

```
probability(catObj=npi_cat, theta = 2, item = 1)
```

```
## [1] 0.8118352
```

```
probability(catObj=npi_cat, theta = -2, item = 1)
```

```
## [1] 0.08030912
```

We see for item 1 that an individual with a higher position on narcissistic dimension has a much higher probability of answering '1' than a person with a lower position on the latent trait. (We discuss identification and how to interpret positive and negative values before concluding this section on page 19.)

We can also plot the entire IRF. Figure 6 plots the IRF for this same item with response options:

- '0': I have a natural talent for influencing people.
- '1': I am not good at influencing people.

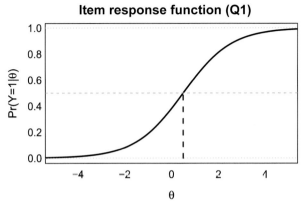

Figure 6 Example item response function for first question in the NPI battery

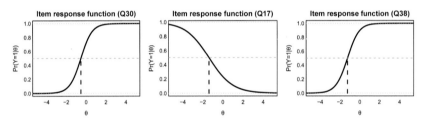

Figure 7 Item response functions for three items

```
plot(npi_cat, item=1, plotType="IRF")
```

The horizontal axis represents θ_j. The vertical axis is the probability of observing a '1' response. So, in this example, a respondent with a $\theta_j = 3$ is very likely to respond with a '1' while the opposite is true for a respondent with $\theta_j = -3$. The vertical dashed line indicates the point in the latent space where respondents have exactly a 50 percent chance of answering in either direction.

This plot helps us understand this specific item, but does not give a good sense of what the item parameters (a_i, b_i) mean more generally. So let's compare several IRFs.

Figure 7 shows three IRFs. Question 30 has a high discrimination parameter $(b = 1.78)$, meaning that the curve is more vertical, but a modest difficulty parameter $(a = 0.95)$, meaning that the vertical movement occurs just below zero. Question 17, by contrast, has a negative discrimination parameter that is closer to zero $(b = -0.867)$, meaning the curve is flatter and is oriented so that individuals with high θ_j values are *less* likely to respond with a '1'. Finally, Question 38 has a very large difficulty parameter $(a = 2.50)$, meaning that the sharp rise in the IRF occurs farther to the left of zero.

As these examples illustrate, the item parameters determine the shape of the IRF curve. The discrimination parameter (b_i) indicates how informative the response is about the latent trait (similar to a factor loading in a factor analysis). Values farther from zero mean that the slope of the curve is increasingly steep. The so-called difficulty parameter (a_i), on the other hand, indicates at what level on the latent trait the item is best targeted. Note that these plots also indicate the position where a respondent is predicted to have exactly a 50 percent chance of answering '1'. This can be calculated analytically as $\frac{-a_i}{b_i}$. This means that higher a_i values are associated with "easier" questions (when b_i is positive). This makes the term "difficulty parameter" more awkward but arises from the fact that we parameterize the IRF slightly differently than some other presentations to stay consistent with the 1tm package. We will stick with the traditional terminology, but it might be useful to think of these as "easiness" parameters since (all things equal) higher values are associated with questions where more people are expected to respond '1'.

A final consideration is that the latent space does not automatically take on a natural meaning. The 1tm package identifies the scale of the latent space by assuming the standard deviation of ability estimates is 1 in the calibration sample. Importantly, however, the 1tmCat function also constrains the first item to have a *positive* discrimination parameter. This affects how we interpret final estimates.

This talk of identification can be a bit confusing, so let's consider the implications of this constraint in our NPI example. The response options for the first questions are: '0' if you feel "I have a natural talent for influencing people" and '1' if you feel "I am not good at influencing people." Since the first item's discrimination parameter is constrained to be positive, this means that a positive position on the latent trait actually indicates *less* narcissism. That is, the meaning of the latent scale is set so that positive values mean you are more likely to say "I am not good at influencing people," and negative values mean you are more likely to say "I have a natural talent for influencing people." If this becomes confusing, the easiest solution is to change the ordering of the questions in your dataset so that responding with a '1' to the first item indicates "more" of the latent trait. Alternatively, you can reverse code the final estimates.

In general, when working with a new battery it is always good practice to visually examine the IRFs to get a sense of how the items work. Computerized adaptive testing algorithms tend to prefer items targeted at the position of the respondent. For example, if the algorithm thinks the respondent is located at $\theta_j = 1$, it will tend to pick items where the dashed red line ($\frac{-a_i}{b_i}$) in the figures is also near 1 (all things equal). Thus, examining the IRFs will tell you which items are likely to be used for respondents at different positions along the latent scale.

2.1.2 Likelihood

The next quantity needed is the *likelihood* of observing the respondents' answers to the survey thus far for any assumed value of θ_j. Letting $P_{ij} = \mathrm{Pr}_i(y_{ij} = 1|\theta_j)$, and $Q_{ij} = 1 - P_{ij}$, the likelihood function associated with the observed response profile $\mathbf{y}_j^{\mathrm{obs}}$ is:

$$
\mathbb{L}(\theta_j|\mathbf{y}_j^{\mathrm{obs}}) = \prod_{i=1}^{n} \left(P_{ij}^{y_{ij}} Q_{ij}^{(1-y_{ij})} \right)
$$

$$
= \exp\left[\sum_{i=1}^{n} \left(y_{ij} \log(P_{ij}) + (1 - y_{ij}) \log(Q_{ij}) \right) \right]. \tag{2}
$$

Consider a scenario in which the items chosen for a respondent were 23, 36, 38, and 21 and she answers '1', '1', '0', '1' (see the help file for question wordings using ?npi). These answers indicate someone who is mildly narcissistic. Given how we identified the scale, we intuitively expect a moderately negative estimate for θ_j.

After assigning these answers in the Cat object, you can calculate the likelihood of observing this response profile given different values of θ_j.

```
ans_profile <- rep(NA, ncol(npi)) # Vector of missing responses
ans_profile[c(23, 36, 38, 21)] <- c(1, 1, 0, 1) # Answers
setAnswers(npi_cat) <- ans_profile # Storing these answers in the Cat object
```

Specifically, we calculate that the likelihood of observing these answers given the respondent's true position on the latent trait is $\theta_j = 2$ (indicating less narcissism), which is much lower than if the respondent's position is $\theta_j = -2$. This result aligns with our expectations.

```
likelihood(npi_cat, theta = 2)   # Calculate the likelihood when theta=2
```

```
## [1] 1.804899e-05
```

```
likelihood(npi_cat, theta = -2) # Calculate the likelihood when theta=-2
```

```
## [1] 0.01435477
```

Figure 8 shows a visualization of Equation 2 for this response profile for different values of θ_j. Visually, it looks like the likelihood function reaches its peak just below -1.

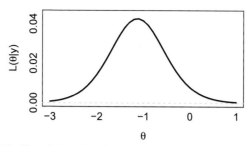

Figure 8 Likelihood function for a respondent who has answered four questions

2.1.3 Prior and Posterior

Several of the item selection algorithms in catSurv adopt a Bayesian frame-work (van der Linden 1998). From this viewpoint, we do not just think about how "likely" some set of responses would be. Instead, we begin with some prior beliefs about respondents' positions on the latent trait and then update our beliefs as new data are collected. The result of combining our prior with the likelihood is termed our posterior beliefs.

In mathematical terms the posterior distribution is:

$$\pi(\theta_j|\mathbf{y}_j^{\text{obs}}) = \frac{\mathbb{L}(\theta_j|\mathbf{y}_j^{\text{obs}})\pi(\theta_j)}{f(\mathbf{y}_j^{\text{obs}})}, \tag{3}$$

where $f(\mathbf{y}_j^{\text{obs}})$ is the marginal distribution of the observed data. Here, $\pi(\theta_j|\mathbf{y}_j^{\text{obs}})$ is the posterior distribution of θ_j. For historical reasons, it is typical to express likelihood functions as $\mathbb{L}(\theta_j|\mathbf{y}_j^{\text{obs}})$. In fact, this is just the joint probability of the data **given** the parameter value $\mathbb{L}(\theta_j|\mathbf{y}_j^{\text{obs}}) = f(\mathbf{y}_j^{\text{obs}}|\theta_j)$, where $f(\cdot)$ is the probability density function (PDF) for the data. Since we will be discussing both Bayesian and maximum likelihood methods in this text, we will stick with former notation.

We have already described the likelihood, so to complete the numerator in Equation 3 we only need to express our prior beliefs, $\pi(\theta_j)$, about the position of θ_j. A standard approach in this literature is simply to assume that all θ_j's are distributed normally around 0. Zero here is the center of the distribution of the θ_j values for the population used to calibrate the IRT model. Having a 0 prior means you are assuming that the new respondents have a similar distribution as the respondents used to fit the model.

Since θ_j is very unlikely in practice to fall outside of the range of −4 to 4, setting the standard deviation for the normal distribution to something near 1.5 usually ensures that all plausible values are given some prior weight. Subsequent sections provide additional discussion of how to choose priors. Note that

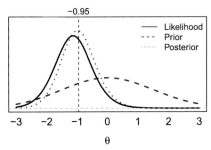

Figure 9 Prior, likelihood, and posterior for one individual respondent

the `ltm` assumes that the θ values are distributed according to a standard normal when estimating the item parameters. In practice, therefore, values beyond four are extremely unlikely. If you fit your IRT model using a different identification assumption, a different prior may be appropriate.

```
# Prior mean of 0 and standard deviation of 1.5
setPriorParams(npi_cat)<-c(0, 1.5)
```

The final step is to calculate the marginal distribution of the data $f(\mathbf{y}_j^{\text{obs}})$. This cannot be done analytically, but it can be approximated with high levels of accuracy by numerically calculating $f(\mathbf{y}_j^{\text{obs}}) = \int_{-\infty}^{\infty} \mathbb{L}(\theta_j|\mathbf{y}_j^{\text{obs}})\pi(\theta_j)d\theta_j$. All integration in `catSurv` is done using the highly precise adaptive quadrature procedure in the GNU scientific library (GSL).

Figure 9 provides a visual depiction of a normal prior distribution (with a mean of 0 and a standard deviation of 1.5), the same likelihood function as depicted in Figure 8, and the resulting posterior. You can see that the posterior is slightly "shrunk" toward zero as a result of also considering the prior. That is, the posterior is just to the right of the likelihood due to the influence of the prior. In some cases, this can result in small amounts of bias in our estimates. However, in many settings working with the posterior rather than the likelihood can have distinct advantages for adaptive tests. We discuss these issues in Section 3.

2.2 Estimating the Respondents' Location: EAP Estimation

We are now in a position to explain the various stages of a standard CAT. The first step is to estimate a respondent's current position on the latent trait. Above, θ_j was a parameter that was passed into the `probability()` and `likelihood()` functions. The goal in `probability()`, for instance, is to see how different positions on the latent trait influence the probability of answering with a '1'.

But now we want to do the reverse – we want to use previous responses to estimate a respondent's position on the latent trait. This is the first step in the CAT algorithm. There are many statistical routines for this task, but for simplicity we will explain just one approach now: expected a posteriori (EAP) estimation.

As the name suggests, the EAP is the expected value of the posterior distribution in Equation 3. Applying the definition of an expected value, we get

$$\mathbb{E}_\theta(\theta_j | \mathbf{y}_j^{obs}) = \frac{\int_{-\infty}^{\infty} \theta_j \mathbb{L}(\theta_j | \mathbf{y}_j^{obs}) \pi(\theta_j) d\theta_j}{\int_{-\infty}^{\infty} \mathbb{L}(\theta_j | \mathbf{y}_j^{obs}) \pi(\theta_j) d\theta_j}, \tag{4}$$

where $\mathbb{L}(\theta_j | \mathbf{y}_j^{obs})$ is again the likelihood of observing the respondent's answer profile as defined previously, and $\pi(\theta_j)$ is the prior. Note that this expectation is taken with respect to θ_j, which in this framework is considered to be a random variable.

The `estimateTheta()` function uses adaptive quadrature methods to approximate these single-dimensional integrals with very high accuracy. Note, however, that it cannot numerically consider all values from $-\infty$ to ∞ and must instead specify bounds for the integration. These are set in the `lowerBound` and `upperBound` slots of the `Cat` object and the default values are -5 and 5. For very extreme individuals on the latent scale, it may be worth expanding these bounds, although it may make item selection slightly slower. Note, however, that for the categorical models discussed in Section 4, expanding the bounds too widely can lead to numerical problems. In fact, if you run into numerical issues, decreasing these bounds to -4 and 4 is our first suggestion.

Recall the scenario described in Section 2.1.2 where a respondent answers questions 23, 36, 38, and 21, a response set we would expect to lead to a moderate narcissism score just below zero. We can calculate our estimate of the respondent's position on the latent trait, $\hat{\theta}_j$, feeding the `estimateTheta()` function our `Cat` object. To indicate that we would like to use the EAP approach, we must edit the `estimation` slot of the `Cat` object. We also need to specify the prior.

```
setEstimation(npi_cat) <- "EAP"
setPriorName(npi_cat) <- "NORMAL"
# Prior mean of 0 and standard deviation of 1.5
setPriorParams(npi_cat) <- c(0,1.5)
estimateTheta(npi_cat)
```

```
## [1] -0.9481451
```

Note that this value is very near the mode of the posterior in Figure 9, but to the right of the mode of the likelihood due to the influence of the prior.

Researchers may also want to quantify uncertainty about this estimate. Applying the definition of variance, the posterior variance for θ_j is:

$$\mathbb{V}\mathrm{ar}(\theta_j) = \mathbb{E}_\theta \left[(\theta_j - \hat{\theta}_j)^2 | \mathbf{y}_j^{\mathrm{obs}} \right] = \frac{\int (\theta_j - \hat{\theta}_j)^2 \mathrm{L}(\theta_j | \mathbf{y}_j^{\mathrm{obs}}) \pi(\theta_j) \mathrm{d}\theta_j}{\int \mathrm{L}(\theta_j | \mathbf{y}_j^{\mathrm{obs}}) \pi(\theta_j) \mathrm{d}\theta_j}, \tag{5}$$

where $\hat{\theta}_j$ is the EAP estimate. The posterior standard deviation is then the square root of this. To be consistent with the maximum likelihood method, we refer to this as the standard error. For the respondent we have created, you can estimate the standard error (or posterior standard deviation) using `estimateSE()`.

```
estimateSE(npi_cat)
```

```
## [1] 0.5933392
```

2.3 Item Selection: Minimum Expected Posterior Variance

Now we come to the heart of the matter. How does CAT go about selecting the next best item to administer to a respondent? While there are many criteria (see, e.g., Choi and Swartz 2009; van der Linden 1998), we will review one here: minimum expected posterior variance (MEPV).

Before getting into the details, however, it is helpful to think through the task intuitively. The goal of the algorithm is to choose the item that will tell us the most about the respondent. This means we want an item that will reduce our uncertainty about the respondent's position, and, in statistical terms, this means we want the item that provides the most information. Or, inversely, we would like to find items that reduce the variance for our estimate of θ_j.

"Information" is a statistical term that can be confusing since it comes in many flavors with many names: Fisher information, observed information, expected information, Kullback–Leibler information, and even expected Kullback–Leibler information. We will try to clarify some of this confusion in the next section. However, the key point for this discussion is that information is inversely related to our estimated variance of θ. Roughly, the more information an item provides, the lower the variance estimate will be. And since reducing uncertainty is our goal, all of the selection criteria we cover aim to choose items that either maximize information or reduce expected variance since they are two sides of the same coin.

So the goal is to choose some item from the set of unasked items. We can divide this problem into two components. First, we choose some criteria we want to optimize. The second problem, however, is that these criteria depend on the unknown parameter θ_j and on the response we *will* get to the questions we might ask, y^*_{ij}. Since we don't know either of these quantities, we have to use our model and the respondent's previous answers to make an informed guess.

We can formalize this a bit within the context of MEPV. In this case, our goal is to minimize the squared distance between our estimate $\hat{\theta}_j$ and the true parameter θ_j, $(\theta_j - \hat{\theta}_j)^2$. Of course we do not know the value of θ_j, but we do have beliefs reflected in the posterior, $\pi(\theta_j | \mathbf{y}^{obs}_j)$. This allows us to find the expected value, $\mathbb{E}_\theta \left[(\theta_j - \hat{\theta}_j)^2 | \mathbf{y}^{obs}_j \right] = \mathbb{V}ar(\theta_j)$, using Equation 5.

However, this quantity only reflects the data we have collected so far. Actually, we want to predict what $\mathbb{V}ar(\theta_j)$ *will be* after the respondent has answered some potential item. We can denote this quantity as $\mathbb{V}ar(\theta_j | y^*_{ij} = 1, \mathbf{y}^{obs}_j)$. But this is now a *probabilistic event* so we need to weight by the probability that $y^*_{ij} = 1$. So, again using our current posterior beliefs about θ_j, we calculate the probability of each possible response. When we combine this together we get the expected posterior variance (EPV):

$$
\text{EPV} = \underbrace{\Pr_i(y^*_{ij} = 1 | \hat{\theta}_j)}_{\text{Prob. of observing 1}} \overbrace{\mathbb{V}ar(\theta_j | y^*_{ij} = 1, \mathbf{y}^{obs}_j)}^{\text{Variance we will have if } y^*_{ij}=1}
$$

$$
+ \underbrace{\Pr_i(y^*_{ij} = 0 | \hat{\theta})}_{\text{Prob. of observing 0}} \overbrace{\mathbb{V}ar(\theta_j | y^*_{ij} = 0, \mathbf{y}^{obs}_j)}^{\text{Variance we will have if } y^*_{ij}=0} . \tag{6}
$$

The first part of Equation 6 is the probability that the respondent will answer '1' (based on the data we have collected so far) times the variance of θ_j we *would have* if she answered '1'. The second part is the probability that the respondent will answer '0' times the variance of θ_j *if* she answered '0'. Altogether, this is our level of uncertainty about θ_j *in expectation*.

Under the hood, CAT calculates this quantity for each (unasked) item in the battery. We then know the expected variance for item 1, item 2, and so on. Then, CAT simply selects the question with the lowest value – the question that will best lower the posterior variance estimate in expectation.

To implement this we specify the MEPV routine in the `selection` slot of the `Cat` object.

```
setSelection(npi_cat) <- "EPV"
```

Next, the function `selectItem` will estimate the EPV for each unasked item. The function returns a list. The first element is a dataframe of the expected posterior variance for each unasked item. The second element is the question number associated with the minimum EPV value – the next best item. The third element is the name of the item (rather than the index).

```
select <- selectItem(npi_cat)
tail(select$estimates) # tail() shows the final rows of a dataframe
```

```
##      q_number q_name       EPV
## 31        33    Q33 0.3044012
## 32        34    Q34 0.3134574
## 33        35    Q35 0.2844596
## 34        37    Q37 0.3308077
## 35        39    Q39 0.3134254
## 36        40    Q40 0.2997187
```

Note that the EPV was not calculated for items 36 and 38 since in this case the respondent has already answered those items.

We can actually rank all items by EPV. Here we list out the top five items in order:

```
## Showing estimates in order of EPV from smallest to largest
head(select$estimates[sort(select$estimates$EPV, index=TRUE)$ix,], 5)
```

```
##      q_number q_name       EPV
## 25        27    Q27 0.2536812
## 30        32    Q32 0.2821062
## 33        35    Q35 0.2844596
## 28        30    Q30 0.2907217
## 9          9     Q9 0.2957515
```

This output shows the EPV calculated for each question item remaining in the battery in increasing order. We can identify the optimal item just by looking at the `next_item` element now stored in the `select` object.

```
select$next_item
```

```
## [1] 27
```

```
select$next_item_name
```

```
## [1] "Q27"
```

This is item 27, where respondents choose between ('0') "I have a strong will to power" and ('1') "Power for its own sake doesn't interest me." To get a sense of why this item was chosen, we can look at the IRF.

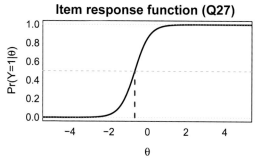

Figure 10 Example item response function for first question in the NPI battery

Figure 10 shows that Q27 is an item where the line dividing individuals expected to answer '1' and those expected to answer '0' is very near our current $\hat{\theta}_j$ (estimated as about −0.95 in Section 2.2). We can also see that the curve is very sharp, indicating it has a high (in absolute terms) discrimination parameter. Intuitively, it is the combination of those factors that makes this item preferable for this respondent.

2.4 Check Stopping Rules

After CAT selects an item, we administer the question to the respondent and record the answer. The next step is determining whether or not to stop asking questions. There are several stopping rules one could choose, but the most basic is a length threshold. That is, once a respondent has answered a predefined number of questions, we should stop asking questions.

Recall our hypothetical respondent has answered four questions. Let's set the length threshold to be five questions and demonstrate that we have not met this stopping rule.

```
setLengthThreshold(npi_cat) <- 5 # Set the threshold
checkStopRules(npi_cat) # Check
```

```
## [1] FALSE
```

Now, we can adaptively administer the next item to our hypothetical respondent, record their answer as '1', and check the stopping rule again.

```
#Calculate the next best item to ask
whichToAsk <- selectItem(npi_cat)$next_item
npi_cat@answers[whichToAsk] <- 1 #Assume respondent chooses option '1'
checkStopRules(npi_cat) # Stopping criteria has now been reached.
```

```
## [1] TRUE
```

At this point, question administration for this respondent would stop.

2.5 Creating Final Estimates

Once you have stopped collecting data, the last step is to provide final estimates. Since different respondents have been given different questions, we cannot use traditional summary statistics. Thinking about this in terms of testing, looking at the number of questions students got right is not useful since CAT intentionally chose questions of differing difficulty levels for different students. You will therefore rely on the original model parameters to estimate respondents' final position on the latent trait.

For a single respondent, we simply use the `estimateTheta()` function However, if the responses are stored in a dataframe (rather than in a Cat object), you can also use the `estimateThetas()` (note the plural) function. The function expects there to be as many columns in the dataset as there are items in the Cat object. So columns for *all* items must be included in the dataframe even if no respondents actually answered some items.

```
FirstFive<-npi[1:5,] # Using responses from the first five observations
estimateThetas(catObj=npi_cat, responses=FirstFive)
```

```
## [1] -0.5751657 1.1037820 -1.3371873 -1.5403242 0.9419209
```

2.6 Application to NPI

Before moving on, let's quickly work through a more concrete example to see if CAT is worth the trouble. Recall that for this example we used only the first 500 respondents to fit our `npi_cat`. So a natural question is, how well can CAT approximate θ_j for some new respondent? Here, we choose respondent 507. (Section 5 provides a more comprehensive approach using multiple respondents.) If we looked at her complete response profile, this respondent chose options including:

- "I have a natural talent for influencing people."
- "If I ruled the world it would be a better place."
- "I like to be the center of attention."

These responses indicate this respondent is highly narcissistic, meaning we expect a large, negative $\hat{\theta}_j$. And based on the *complete* response profile to all 40 questions, we indeed find that $\hat{\theta}_j = -2.799$

```
npi_cat@answers<-unlist(npi[507,]) # unlist() to remove data.frame class
estimateTheta(catObj=npi_cat)
```
```
## [1] -2.799175
```

Now we can reset the `answers` slot of our Cat object and imagine we have no answers from this respondent.

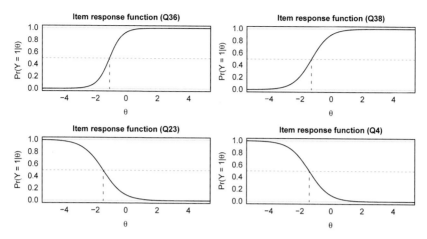

Figure 11 Item response functions for four items

```
npi_cat@answers<-rep(NA, 40)
```

Again, our goal is to see how close we can get to this estimate using a much shorter adaptive battery. With a simple `while` loop, we can administer a five-item AI. That is, we will use the *recorded* responses from this respondent to fill in their response profile until we get to five total answers.

```
shouldStop<-FALSE
while(shouldStop==FALSE){
  ask_this<-selectItem(catObj = npi_cat)$next_item # Choose item
  print(ask_this) # Show the questions that were chosen
  npi_cat<-storeAnswer(npi_cat, item = ask_this,
                  answer=npi[507,ask_this]) # Store observed response
  shouldStop<-checkStopRules(npi_cat) # Check stop rule
}
```

```
## [1] 27
## [1] 36
## [1] 23
## [1] 4
## [1] 38
```

We see that the algorithm chose items 27, 36, 23, 4, and 38, in that order. In each case, the respondent chose the response that indicated higher levels of narcissism. We gain intuition by again looking at IRFs for these items. Item 27 is shown at Figure 10, and Figure 11 shows the remaining items.

We see that they all have fairly high discrimination parameters and target individuals far to left of zero. Moreover, the battery starts with more moderate items and chooses increasingly extreme items (although this pattern is not strict). With these responses, our $\hat{\theta}_j$ estimate is:

```
estimateTheta(catObj=npi_cat) # Not Bad!
```

```
## [1] -2.531489
```

Thus, our final estimate (made using only 5 questions) differs from the estimate we would get using the complete battery (using 40 questions) by only 0.25.

This is just one example for one respondent, but as we show later, these results generalize. When we have a well-calibrated CAT model, an AI can approximate estimates from a much longer battery using a fraction of the survey time. We provide more evidence for this claim in Section 5. However, next, we turn to alternative implementations of CAT.

3 Exploring Your Options: Alternative CAT Algorithms

In the previous sections, we provided a broad overview of adaptive inventories and some intuition about how and why they work. This section walks through additional options for implementing CAT algorithms and also gets into the "guts" of the various routines.

Sections 3 and 4 are the most technical parts of this Element. Our aim is to succinctly summarize the details for all of the basic routines you might want. This more formal presentation also serves as a way to discuss some of the conceptual differences among methods and is a reference you can return to if you encounter problems.

The `catSurv` software contains options covering multiple flavors of CAT algorithms. Figure 12 shows a complete list. Researchers can choose between four different response models, four ability estimation methods, ten item selection routines, and multiple stopping rules. Even this somewhat overwhelming list represents only a small subset of the variations available in the broader literature. However, we feel that these options offer a sufficient set of tools for most applications in the survey domain. This section provides a broad overview of these options, their purpose, and some intuitions as to how they differ.

At this point readers may be wondering, "which method is best?" But it is impossible to give a general answer to that question. It will depend on your specific battery, the number of items you wish to use, and more. We tend to prefer EAP estimation and MEPV selection as they seem to work well and encounter fewer numerical issues. But there are many cases when alternative methods may be preferred.

Although we cannot supply a concrete answer to this question, we do provide extensive tools to help researchers consider and evaluate their options in

Model
   Two-parameter item response model
   Birnbum's three-parameter model
   Graded response model
   Generalized partial credit model
Prior structures
   Normal
   T-distribution
   Uniform
Item selection criterion
   Maximum Fisher's information
   Kullback-Leibler
   Likelihood weighted Kullback-Leibler
   Posterior weighted Kullback-Leibler
   Maximum likelihood weighted Fisher's information
   Maximum posterior weighted Fisher's information
   Maximum expected information criterion
   Minimum expected posterior variance
   Maximum Fisher interval information
   Random

Stopping rule
   Length
   Precision
   Information
   Gain
Stopping rule override
   Length
   Gain
θ **estimation**
   Maximum likelihood
   Weighted likelihood
   Expected a posteriori
   Maximum a posteriori

Figure 12 Primary options in the `catSurv` package

Section 5. In addition, Section 4 discusses models for categorical outcomes. Several other models are actually special cases of the four models listed in Figure 12 and `catSurv` can accommodate them. For instance, the rating scale model is a special case of the partial credit model.

The rest of this section is structured as follows. We begin by introducing an example and then discuss prior structures, θ estimation, item selection, and stopping rules. Finally, Section 3.6 introduces a variation of the binary model that allows for guessing. The presentation of the model and algorithm options in this section largely follows the presentation in van der Linden and Pashley (2010) and depends heavily on results in Baker and Kim (2004).

3.1 Measuring Knowledge

To motivate this section, we return to our example from Section 1 where we administered multiple-choice political knowledge questions to a convenience sample. In this case, we first fit the model directly in the `ltm` package and then pass the result to `ltmCat()`. We do this to specify additional parameters for the `ltm` measurement model (e.g., we use the `nlminb` optimizer).

```
data(polknowMT)
ltm_fit <- ltm::ltm(polknowMT~z1, start.val="random",
            control = list(optimizer = "nlminb"))
ltm_cat <- ltmCat(ltm_fit) # Passing an existing ltm model as an argument
```

3.2 Likelihood and Prior Distributions

Early approaches to CAT were almost exclusively based on maximum likelihood estimation (MLE). Later, a number of Bayesian methods appeared. More confusingly, some approaches to CAT mix them together, using priors when necessary but maintaining a philosophical commitment to MLE. We will not revisit the philosophical differences between MLE and Bayesian inference here. However, it is helpful to emphasize some distinctions.

Both approaches begin by assuming that the observed data come from a known model. Specifically, we assume the data are drawn out of a Bernoulli distribution,

$$\mathbf{y}_j^{\text{obs}} \overset{iid}{\sim} \text{Bernoulli}\Big(\text{Pr}_i(y_{ij} = 1|\theta_j)\Big),$$

where the probability of a '1' is $\text{Pr}_i(y_{ij} = 1|\theta_j)$. For brevity, we sometimes refer to this as P_{ij} and let $P_{ij} = 1 - Q_{ij}$. Where we wish to emphasize the dependence on θ_j, we will write $P_i(\theta_j) = 1 - Q_i(\theta_j)$. The *iid* indicates that observed responses are independent and identically distributed once we have conditioned on θ_j. That is, patterns in responses across items are assumed to be driven exclusively by the respondent's position on the latent trait.

With this notation, the joint probability of any set of observed responses is shown in Equation 2 and is called the likelihood. The MLE approach to CAT aims to base inferences and item selection only on the likelihood. In this framework, it is the data (our sample) that are the random variables. Our only uncertainty comes from the sampling distribution of the MLE, $\hat{\theta}_j$. For MLE approaches, therefore, we emphasize that expectations are taken with respect to the data with the notation $\mathbb{E}_y(\cdot)$.

The Bayesian approach relies on the same likelihood but is philosophically quite different. Here, we begin with prior beliefs about the unknown parameter itself, θ_j. We assume that we can express these beliefs as a probability distribution $\pi(\theta_j)$. Our aim, therefore, is to *update* our beliefs according to Bayes rule as shown in Equation 3. In this setting, it is the parameter (or perhaps our beliefs about the parameter) that are the random variable. For Bayesian approaches, therefore, we emphasize that expectations are taken with respect to the parameter with the notation $\mathbb{E}_\theta(\cdot)$.

In some settings, these differences do not amount to much. To begin with, the posterior and likelihood will lead to nearly identical choices if we choose "vague" priors (e.g., the uniform prior). Further, the prior can be swamped by the likelihood given even reasonably sized data sets. But in CAT, prior selection can matter since $\mathbf{y}_j^{\text{obs}}$ represents one person's observed responses and is typically small. Thus, our final estimates and the items we choose will often be a function of prior choices.

The `catSurv` software allows users to choose from three different families of prior distributions: the normal distribution, the Student's *t*-distribution, and the uniform distribution. Moreover, researchers can select the appropriate parameters for each. Both the distribution and the parameters are set using the `setPriorName()` and `setPriorParams()` function.

```
setPriorName(ltm_cat)<-"NORMAL"
setPriorParams(ltm_cat)<-c(0,1.6) # Mean = 0; SD=1.6
prior(catObj=ltm_cat, theta=2) # Height of prior distribution at theta=2
```

```
## [1] 0.1141557
```

For each family of priors, the parameters take on different interpretations. For the normal distribution, the parameters indicate the mean and standard deviation. For the *t*-distribution, the parameters indicate, first, where the distribution should be centered and, second, the degrees of freedom. Note that larger values for the second parameter (the degrees of freedom) indicate narrower prior beliefs. Finally, for the uniform distribution, the parameters indicate the leftmost and rightmost limits. A plot of four different prior distributions is shown in the left panel of Figure 13.

How do we decide which prior to use? To discuss this, we create an example case where a respondent has answered three questions. The posterior distribution that results for this data with each prior is shown in the right panel of Figure 13.

```
ans_profile <- rep(NA, 64) # Vector of missing responses
ans_profile[c(1, 2, 20)] <- c(1, 0, 0) # Answers for the chosen items
setAnswers(ltm_cat) <- ans_profile # Storing these answers in the Cat object
```

Each prior has its own advantages and disadvantages. The normal prior is familiar and results in nicely shaped posteriors. However, the standard normal prior (with standard deviation equal to 1) tends to shrink the posterior distribution noticeably toward zero. With binary data, we recommend setting the standard deviation to 1.6 or 1.8. The *t*-distribution priors have the nice property of fatter "tails," so the resulting posterior distribution tends to be more informed by the data. However, the posterior variance estimates for θ_j are somewhat wider for this same reason. Finally, the uniform prior will result in a posterior that *exactly* mimics the likelihood within the bounds and will be zero otherwise.

Intuitively, therefore, the priors should be selected depending on whether we want the algorithm to adjust quickly to new data or to be a bit more conservative. The less informative priors (e.g., uniform) will change $\hat{\theta}_j$ estimates quickly while the normal priors will wait for more evidence. It is

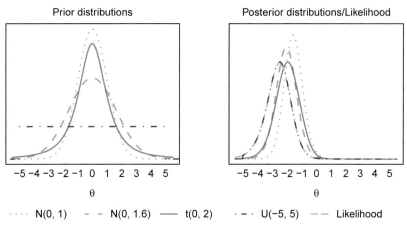

Figure 13 Alternative prior distributions for θ and resulting posterior distributions

impossible to say which is better in all settings, but you can test out different options using the simulation tools described in Section 5.

3.3 Estimating θ

Section 2 described how to find the expected a posteriori estimate of θ. The catSurv package includes three other options: maximum likelihood estimation (MLE), modal a posteriori estimation (MAP), and weighted maximum likelihood estimation (WLE).

From a practical standpoint, these algorithms are all simple to use. Just specify your preferred estimation method and use the function estimateTheta(). However, there are a few common problems that are hard to grasp without a better understanding of how the algorithm actually works.

3.3.1 MLE and MAP

For MLE and MAP, catSurv implements a standard Newton-Rhapson algorithm that essentially "climbs the hill" by using the first and second derivatives of the log-likelihood functions or log-posteriors (see ?d1LL and ?d2LL for additional details). We first define the log-likelihood as

$$\lambda(\theta_j|\mathbf{y}_j^{obs}) \equiv \log \mathbb{L}(\theta_j|\mathbf{y}_j^{obs}). \tag{7}$$

We can take the first and second derivatives

$$\frac{\mathrm{d}\lambda}{\mathrm{d}\theta_j} = \frac{\partial \log \mathbb{L}(\theta_j|\mathbf{y}_j^{obs})}{\partial \theta_j}, \quad \frac{\mathrm{d}^2\lambda}{\mathrm{d}\theta_j^2} = \frac{\partial^2 \log \mathbb{L}(\theta_j|\mathbf{y}_j^{obs})}{\partial \theta_j^2}. \tag{8}$$

The exact formulas for each are shown in the Section 3.7. With a normal prior on $\theta_j \sim N(\mu_\theta, \sigma_\theta^2)$, we can follow a similar procedure for the numerator of the log-posteriors,

$$\rho(\theta_j | \mathbf{y}_j^{\text{obs}}) \equiv \log \mathbb{L}(\theta_j | \mathbf{y}_j^{\text{obs}}) + \log \pi(\theta). \tag{9}$$

This results in

$$\frac{d\rho}{d\theta_j} = \frac{\partial \log \mathbb{L}(\theta_j | \mathbf{y}_j^{\text{obs}})}{\partial \theta_j} - \frac{\theta_j - \mu_\theta}{\sigma_\theta^2}, \quad \frac{d^2\rho}{d\theta_j^2} = \frac{\partial^2 \log \mathbb{L}(\theta_j | \mathbf{y}_j^{\text{obs}})}{\partial \theta_j^2} - \frac{1}{\sigma_\theta^2}. \tag{10}$$

The algorithm iteratively applies Equation 11 to find values of θ that will maximize the likelihood (for MLE). (For the three-parameter model discussed later, this might be better labeled Fisher-scoring.) To find the mode of the posterior (MAP), we simply replace λ with ρ. That is, it starts with some guess (usually $\theta_j = 0$) about the value of $\hat{\theta}_j$ and then "updates" the estimate according to

$$[\hat{\theta}_j]_{(t+1)} = [\hat{\theta}_j]_{(t)} - \left[\frac{d\lambda}{d\theta_j} \Big/ \frac{d^2\lambda}{d\theta_j^2} \right]. \tag{11}$$

It repeats this until $\hat{\theta}_{(t+1)} \approx \hat{\theta}_{(t)}$, which usually takes only three or four iterations. In some cases, the initial starting value for the algorithm can result in poor convergence if it occurs in areas where the likelihood or posterior are extremely flat. If this occurs, catSurv will try alternative starting values, although convergence cannot be absolutely guaranteed. See chapter 3.2 in Baker and Kim (2004) for additional details. If this happens repeatedly, we suggest switching to the EAP estimation method.

Based on this discussion, it may seem that the MLE and MAP estimators are roughly equivalent. In practice, however, there are important distinctions. The advantage of the MLE approach is that all inferences are based on the data; the results are not influenced by the prior distribution at all. This seems to be the most agnostic approach, and makes the algorithm very responsive to observed answers. However, this extreme responsiveness means that the MLE estimates can be unstable.

Consider, for instance, the case where a respondent answers items 1, 2, and 20 incorrectly. Figure 14 shows the prior, likelihood, and posterior distribution. In this case, the likelihood function continues to increase as θ_j goes down; the MLE is actually $-\infty$. The Bayesian estimates, however, are finite and better behaved thanks to the prior information that indicates that values of θ_j lower than -4 are extremely unlikely. This means that both the MAP and EAP estimates are low but clearly bounded. In general, we recommend EAP estimation, and to a lesser extent MAP estimation, as a default approach.

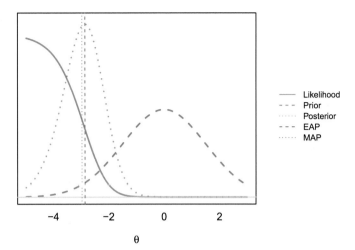

Figure 14 Disadvantages of MLE in adaptive questioning

The tendency of the MLE to run to extreme values is not a mere technical objection. This problem will occur at least once for *every* respondent after they answer their first question (at that point they will have gotten all of their questions right or wrong). Even worse, before respondents answer any questions, the likelihood isn't even defined, which means we can't estimate θ_j at all. To solve this problem, Cat objects are specified with estimation defaults that can be altered using setEstimationDefault(). This is the estimation method that catSurv will rely on when choosing the first item or when the true MLE is $-\infty$, ∞, or undefined. That is, in these instances catSurv will not use MLE estimates at all but rather the default.

3.3.2 Weighted Maximum Likelihood

An often-overlooked fact is that MLE estimates of θ are biased – especially when survey takers have only taken a small number of items. Warm (1989) proposed an alternative estimator that corrects for this bias. The mathematical details are shown in Section 3.7. Practically this can be done using:

```
setEstimation(ltm_cat) <- "WLE"
estimateTheta(ltm_cat)
```

```
## [1] -2.444692
```

Numerically, finding the WLE is somewhat trickier since it involves finding the maximum of a function with (potentially) multiple modes. catSurv does this by using the "Brent" method of root finding in the GSL C++ library. We have found that the WLE estimation method is somewhat more likely to result in computational errors and advise that it only be used for a battery that has been pretested thoroughly.

3.3.3 Fisher Information and Measures of Uncertainty

Basic MLE theory (Pawitan 2001) shows that the limiting distribution for $\hat{\theta}_j$ is informally,

$$\hat{\theta}_j \sim N\left(\theta_j, \mathbb{I}(\theta_j)^{-1}\right), \tag{12}$$

where

$$\mathbb{I}(\theta_j) = -\mathbb{E}_y\left(\frac{d^2\lambda}{d\theta_j^2}\right). \tag{13}$$

This is traditionally referred to as the Fisher information (FI). For the two-parameter binary model the FI is

$$\mathbb{I}(\theta_j) = \sum_i^n b_i^2\left(P_i(\theta_j)Q_i(\theta_j)\right). \tag{14}$$

This is sometimes referred to as the *test information*, since it reflects all of the items administered to a respondent. Thus, to find the variance for the MLE, we simply calculate the inverse of the test information.

Since θ_j is an input for $\mathbb{I}(\theta_j)$, we will estimate the variance for the MLE simply by "plugging in" the MLE for θ_j, $\mathbb{I}(\hat{\theta}_j)^{-1}$. That is, we calculate $P_i(\theta_j)$ and $Q_i(\theta_j)$ by assuming $\theta_j = \hat{\theta}_j$.

We also approximate the variance for the WLE as $\mathbb{I}(\hat{\theta}_j)^{-1}$. The MAP is similar except that there is also uncertainty due to the prior variance term σ_θ^2 (which requires that the prior variance be normal). Specifically, it is $\left(\mathbb{I}(\hat{\theta}_j) + 1/\sigma_\theta^2\right)^{-1}$. MAP estimation relies on Laplace approximation of the posterior, which has similar large-sample properties to the MLE.

In any case, calculating the uncertainty for a θ_j parameter is always done with the estimateSE() function.

```
setEstimation(ltm_cat)<-"MLE"; estimateSE(ltm_cat)
```

```
## [1] 0.7457107
```

```
setEstimation(ltm_cat)<-"MAP"; estimateSE(ltm_cat)
```

```
## [1] 0.661347
```

Note that using the MAP estimator also shrinks standard error estimates. This is again because the prior information stabilizes the posterior distribution for θ_j.

Importantly, $\mathbb{I}(\theta_j)$ can be decomposed into additive units representing the reduction in uncertainty associated with each item. That is, $\mathbb{I}(\theta_j)$ can be decomposed into $\sum_{i=1}^{n} \mathbb{I}_i(\theta_j)$ where

$$\mathbb{I}_i(\theta_j) = b_i^2 \left(P_i(\theta_j) Q_i(\theta_j) \right). \tag{15}$$

Holding b_i constant, this quantity is maximized where $P_{ij} = Q_{ij} = 0.5$, meaning we get the most information at values for θ_j where a respondent is equally likely to respond '0' or '1'.

3.4 Item Selection

The next step is to actually choose items from the broader inventory. Recall from Section 2 that the basic approach is to evaluate each unasked item on some criteria and then choose the item that maximizes (or minimizes) that criteria. Section 2 explained how this works using the MEPV criteria. Table 1 provides an overview of all the options available in `catSurv`. Random item selection is a final method and is useful for simulation exercises.

3.4.1 A General Framework for Understanding Item Selection

Table 1 is a blizzard of notation that nontechnical users may find baffling. In fact, these selection routines are all variations on a theme and share an underlying logic. Broadly, the goal of each item selection method is to choose items that will minimize some loss function. Imagine some respondent j whose true position on the latent trait is denoted θ_j. Further assume we have some battery of items where $\mathbf{y}_j$ represents the **complete** set of responses respondent j would make if asked all items, and $\mathcal{B}$ is the set of possible items and has n elements.

We want to choose some subset of items, $S_j \subset \mathcal{B}$, where the number of elements in S_j is $s < n$. With this notation, we can define some function $\mathcal{L}(S_j | \theta_j, \mathbf{y_j})$, which represents the loss in terms of accuracy or efficiency from using the subset of items S_j instead of the complete set $\mathcal{B}$ given both the respondent's true position and the answers she would give to the complete battery. The optimal reduced battery, therefore, chooses S_j to minimize this loss for respondent j.

There are two problems with following this strategy. To begin, in the ideal case this amounts to choosing the "best" set of items from all $\binom{n}{s}$ possible reduced batteries of length s. For small batteries this might be feasible, but even for modestly sized batteries this is intractable. For example, finding the best 8-item battery chosen from a 40-item battery would involved ranking $\binom{40}{8} \approx 76$ million scales for *each* respondent. A more fundamental problem,

Table 1 Item selection criteria

Method		Abbreviation
Maximum Fisher's information	$\underset{i}{\operatorname{argmax}}\left\{\mathbb{I}_i(\hat{\theta}_j)\right\}$	MFI
Maximum Fisher interval information	$\underset{i}{\operatorname{argmax}}\left\{\int_{\hat{\theta}-\delta}^{\hat{\theta}+\delta}\mathbb{I}_i(\theta_j)\mathrm{d}\theta\right\}$	MFII
Maximum likelihood weighted information	$\underset{i}{\operatorname{argmax}}\left\{\int_{-\infty}^{\infty}\mathbb{L}(\theta_j|\mathbf{y}_j^{\mathrm{obs}})\mathbb{I}_i(\theta_j)\mathrm{d}\theta\right\}$	MLWI
Maximum posterior weighted information	$\underset{i}{\operatorname{argmax}}\left\{\int_{-\infty}^{\infty}\mathbb{L}(\theta_j|\mathbf{y}_j^{\mathrm{obs}})\pi(\theta_j)\mathbb{I}_i(\theta_j)\mathrm{d}\theta\right\}$	MPWI
Maximum expected information	$\underset{i}{\operatorname{argmax}}\left\{\Pr_i(y_{ij}^*=1|\hat{\theta}_j)\mathrm{J}(\theta_j|y_{ij}^*=1,\mathbf{y}_j^{\mathrm{obs}})\right.$ $\left.+\Pr_i(y_{ij}^*=0|\hat{\theta}_j)\mathrm{J}(\theta_j|y_{ij}^*=0,\mathbf{y}_j^{\mathrm{obs}})\right\}$	MEI
Maximum expected Kullback-Leibler information	$\underset{i}{\operatorname{argmax}}\left\{\int_{\hat{\theta}-\delta}^{\hat{\theta}+\delta}\mathrm{EKL}_i\left(\hat{\theta}_j;\theta_j\right)\mathrm{d}\theta_j\right\}$	KL
Maximum likelihood weighted KL information	$\underset{i}{\operatorname{argmax}}\left\{\int_{-\infty}^{\infty}\mathbb{L}(\theta_j|\mathbf{y}_j^{\mathrm{obs}})\mathrm{EKL}_i\left(\hat{\theta}_j;\theta_j\right)\mathrm{d}\theta_j\right\}$	LKL
Maximum posterior weighted KL information	$\underset{i}{\operatorname{argmax}}\left\{\int_{-\infty}^{\infty}\mathbb{L}(\theta_j|\mathbf{y}_j^{\mathrm{obs}})\pi(\theta_j)\mathrm{EKL}_i\left(\hat{\theta}_j;\theta_j\right)\mathrm{d}\theta_j\right\}$	PKL
Minimum expected posterior variance	$\underset{i}{\operatorname{argmin}}\left\{\Pr_i(y_{ij}^*=1|\hat{\theta}_j)\mathbb{V}\mathrm{ar}(\theta_j|y_{ij}^*=1,\mathbf{y}_j^{\mathrm{obs}})\right.$ $\left.+\Pr_i(y_{ij}^*=0|\theta_j)\mathbb{V}\mathrm{ar}(\theta_j|y_{ij}^*=0,\mathbf{y}_j^{\mathrm{obs}})\right\}$	EPV

Note: $\delta=z(\mathbb{I}(\hat{\theta}))^{-1/2}$

however, is that we do not observe the respondent's true position (θ_j) or complete response set ($\mathbf{y}_j$), so we cannot actually calculate $\mathcal{L}(\mathcal{S}_j|\theta_j,\mathbf{y}_j)$ for any battery at all.

To reduce the computational complexity, all item selection routines we consider follow a "greedy" strategy, meaning they choose one item at a time rather than the complete set $\mathcal{S}_j$. That is, at each stage these algorithms consider which question to add *next* to S_j instead of considering all possible reduced batteries. While suboptimal, greedy algorithms are quite common in computer science and statistics and are used in, for instance, random forests models.

The second issue – that we do not observe $(\theta_j, \mathbf{y}_j)$ – is handled differently by the various item selection routines listed in Table 1. Some routines (e.g., MFI) bypass the problem by assuming that our current estimate of θ_j is correct and simply ignoring our uncertainty about $\mathbf{y}_j$. But most try to make educated guesses about θ_j and/or $\mathbf{y}_j$ in choosing the next item.

Broadly speaking, the item selection criteria we discuss differ based on three factors.

1. They differ in how they want to evaluate the quality of the final estimate (the loss function). The primary division here is whether to use Fisher information or Kullback-Leibler information.
2. They differ as to how they make educated guesses about potential values of θ_j.
3. They differ as to whether they also take into account uncertainty about the unobserved response to item i (the item being evaluated), which we denote y_{ij}^*.

With this framework in mind, let us return to the MEPV criteria discussed in Section 2. This will help solidify the basic concepts using a selection routine we already understand. Recall that we have a respondent who has already answered items 1, 2, and 20. We will denote these observed responses as $\mathbf{y}_j^{\text{obs}}$. Our goal is to choose from the remaining 17 items for this respondent.

For MEPV, we specify our loss as $\mathcal{L}(S_j|\theta_j, \mathbf{y}_j) = (\hat{\theta}_j - \theta_j)^2$. Of course, we don't know θ_j. In this Bayesian framework, however, we can simply calculate the expected value with respect to the posterior distribution of θ_j conditioned on their unobserved response to potential item i, y_{ij}^*. Applying the definition of the expected value, we get:

$$\mathbb{E}_\theta\left((\hat{\theta}_j - \theta_j)^2\right) = \int_{-\infty}^{\infty} (\hat{\theta}_j - \theta_j)\pi(\theta_j|\mathbf{y}_j^{\text{obs}}, y_{ij}^*)d\theta_j.$$

The final issue is that we do not know y_{ij}^*, so we instead use $\mathbb{E}(y_{ij}^*|\hat{\theta}, \mathbf{y}_j^{\text{obs}}) = \text{Pr}_i(y_{ij}^* = 1|\hat{\theta}_j)$. This results in the expected posterior variance shown in Table 1.

For our example respondent, we can calculate the EPV for each unasked item in the battery.

```
setEstimation(ltm_cat)<-"EAP"
setSelection(ltm_cat)<-"EPV"
```

```
select<-selectItem(ltm_cat)
select$next_item
```

[1] 3

This shows that, for this respondent, the next best item to select will be item 3.

3.4.2 Fisher Information and Observed Information

In Section 3.3.3 we showed that there is an inverse relationship between test information and the uncertainty for MLE estimates of θ_j. One intuitive approach, therefore, would be to let the loss function for item selection be $\mathcal{L}(S_j|\theta_j, \mathbf{y}_i) = -\mathbb{I}(\theta_j)$. Since $\mathbb{I}(\theta_j)$ is strictly additive across items, all we need to do is choose the item that will maximize $\mathbb{I}_i(\theta_j)$ (note the i subscript).

Of course, we cannot directly evaluate this quantity since we don't know θ_j. The simplest approach is to assume that $\theta_j = \hat{\theta}_j$. This results in the maximum Fisher's information (MFI) criteria:

$$\underset{i}{\mathrm{argmax}} \left\{ \mathbb{I}_i(\hat{\theta}_j) \right\}. \tag{16}$$

This says that we choose the item i that results in the largest FI given our current estimate $\hat{\theta}_j$. For our respondent who has already answered items 1, 2, and 20, we get:

```
# Use MAP as it is more consistent with an MLE approach
setEstimation(ltm_cat)<-"MAP"
setSelection(ltm_cat)<-"MFI"
select<-selectItem(ltm_cat)
select$next_item
```

[1] 3

You can understand this result better by looking at the item information curve (IIC) for item 3 in Figure 15. This shows $\mathbb{I}_i(\theta_j)$ for different values of θ_j. Here we can see that the information for this item is maximized near the MLE and MAP estimators reported in Figure 14 in Section 3.3.1.

The MFI criteria calculates the information only at our current estimate of $\hat{\theta}_j$. Another approach is to evaluate the information on some interval right around $\hat{\theta}_j$. Intuitively, this is like finding the average value of $\mathbb{I}_i(\theta_j)$ for all possible values of θ_j within the interval $\hat{\theta} \pm \delta$. Formally, the maximum Fisher interval information (MFII) approach chooses items as:

$$\underset{i}{\mathrm{argmax}} \left\{ \int_{\hat{\theta}_j - \delta}^{\hat{\theta}_j + \delta} \mathbb{I}_i(\theta_j) \mathrm{d}\theta_j \right\} \tag{17}$$

Item information function

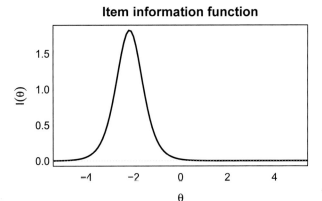

Figure 15 Item information curve for item 3

where $\delta = z(\mathbb{I}(\hat{\theta}))^{-1/2}$, and z is a user specified z-value. In essence, we are assuming that values of θ within z standard errors around $\hat{\theta}_j$ are equally plausible. The default is $z = 1.96$, which approximates a 95 percent confidence interval. That is, we find the value for all θ_j values within 1.96 standard errors of $\hat{\theta}_j$ and use the average. See ?Cat-class for information on the z parameter as well as the setZ() function.

Note that the integration bounds themselves here are defined by $\hat{\theta}_j$ and $\mathbb{I}(\hat{\theta}_j)$. This makes it hard to use when the likelihood is undefined. For the first item, catSurv will therefore default to EPV item selection even if MFII is selected. This same problem (and same solution) holds for the MLWI, KL, and LKL criteria we will discuss below. To avoid this issue, researchers can specify the first item manually.

The MFII approach considers all values of θ_j within that interval to be equally likely. This misses the advantage of having the likelihood and posterior that are intended to reflect the plausibility of various values of θ_j. The maximum likelihood weighted information (MLWI) weights potential values of θ_j by the height of the likelihood curve:

$$\operatorname*{argmax}_i \left\{ \int_{-\infty}^{\infty} \mathbb{L}(\theta_j)\mathbb{I}_i(\theta_j)\mathrm{d}\theta_j \right\}. \tag{18}$$

The maximum posterior weighted information (MPWI) does the same, but also considers the prior when evaluating plausible values for θ_j. Computationally, we cannot integrate across all values, therefore, catSurv integrates across a specified interval of plausible θ_j values specified by lowerBound and upperBound. If you experience numerical issues or get warnings using these methods, we suggest narrowing these intervals.

In most cases, MPWI and MLWI will only generate different recommendations in cases where the posterior and likelihood have dramatically different shapes. In our running example, however, they provide the same recommendation.

```
setSelection(ltm_cat)<-"MLWI"; select<-selectItem(ltm_cat)
select$next_item
```

```
## [1] 3
```

```
setSelection(ltm_cat)<-"MPWI"; select<-selectItem(ltm_cat)
select$next_item
```

```
## [1] 3
```

A final extension in this family is (confusingly) called maximum expected information (MEI). To understand MEI, it is necessary to take a deeper look at the concept of information. In a standard maximum likelihood setting, we can calculate the *observed information* as the negative of the second derivative of the log-likelihood. We will denote this quantity as:

$$J(\theta_j|\mathbf{y}_j^{\text{obs}}) = -\frac{\mathrm{d}^2\lambda}{\mathrm{d}\theta_j^2}. \tag{19}$$

Fisher information is defined as the expected value of this quantity:

$$\mathbb{I}(\theta_j) = \mathbb{E}_y\left(J(\theta_j|\mathbf{y}_j^{\text{obs}})\right). \tag{20}$$

Thus, $\mathbb{I}(\theta_j)$ does not depend on the actual responses since the data itself has been integrated out. In the two-parameter binary model, this distinction is irrelevant because $\frac{\mathrm{d}^2\lambda}{\mathrm{d}\theta_j^2}$ does not involve the data. However, it will come into play for the categorical models in the next section.

The maximum expected information (MEI) criteria is actually based on the *observed information* we will get once the respondent has answered item i, which we can denote $J(\theta_j|\mathbf{y}_j^{\text{obs}}, y_{ij}^*)$. That is, the "expectation" in the name refers to the unobserved observation y_{ij}^*. In essence, since we do not know y_{ij}^* we calculate:

$$\underset{i}{\operatorname{argmax}}\left\{\underbrace{\Pr_i(y_{ij}^*=1|\hat{\theta}_j)}_{\text{Prob. of observing 1}}\overbrace{J(\theta_j|\mathbf{y}_j^{\text{obs}},y_{ij}^*=1)}^{\text{Observed inf. if } y_{ij}^*=1}+\underbrace{\Pr_i(y_{ij}^*=0|\hat{\theta}_j)}_{\text{Prob. of observing 0}}\overbrace{J(\theta_j|\mathbf{y}_j^{\text{obs}},y_{ij}^*=0)}^{\text{Observed inf. if } y_{ij}^*=0}\right\}. \tag{21}$$

3.4.3 Kullback-Leibler Information

Another set of item selection routines derives from the field of statistical information theory, where we replace the Fisher information with the Kullback-Leibler (KL) information (Chang and Ying 1996). Following our schema for understanding item selection, in this approach we set $\mathcal{L}(S_j|\theta_j, \mathbf{y}_i) = -\text{logLR}_i(\hat{\theta}_j; \theta_j)$, where

$$\text{logLR}_i(\hat{\theta}_j; \theta_j) = \log \frac{\mathbb{L}(\theta_j|y_{ij}^*)}{\mathbb{L}(\hat{\theta}_j|y_{ij}^*)} \tag{22}$$

is the log of the likelihood ratio for the true value of θ_j and our current estimate of $\hat{\theta}_j$.

To understand this quantity, we can think about the case where $y_{ij}^* = 1$. Using the definition of the likelihood for this model and the log rules, we would then get $\text{logLR}_i(\hat{\theta}_j; \theta_j) = \log(P_i(\theta_j)) - \log(P_i(\hat{\theta}_j))$. This quantity will be large when the probability of $y_{ij}^* = 1$ is *actually* very high, but our current estimate $\hat{\theta}_j$ would tell us that this probability is very low. In essence, the $\text{logLR}_i(\hat{\theta}_j; \theta_j)$ is high when the response pattern predicted from the true data-generating process (θ_j) would be a surprise to us based on our current point estimate ($\hat{\theta}_j$). The intuition is that such surprising observations move our current estimate toward the true θ_j quickly. Importantly, this divergence is not symmetric, so $KL(\hat{\theta}_j; \theta_j) \neq KL(\theta_j; \hat{\theta}_j)$.

The problem is again that we do not actually know y_{ij}^* or θ_j. To solve the first problem, we adopt the same weighting strategy as for the MEI and MEPV techniques described in Section 3.4.2. This leads to the somewhat confusing name of expected Kullback-Leibler information criteria, where the expectation is taken with respect to y_{ij}^*.

$$\text{EKL}_i(\hat{\theta}_j; \theta_j) = \Pr_i(y_{ij}^* = 1|\theta_j) \log \left[\frac{\Pr_i(y_{ij}^* = 1|\theta_j)}{\Pr_i(y_{ij}^* = 1|\hat{\theta}_j)} \right]$$
$$+ \Pr_i(y_{ij}^* = 0|\theta_j) \log \left[\frac{\Pr_i(y_{ij}^* = 0|\theta_j)}{\Pr_i(y_{ij}^* = 0|\hat{\theta}_j)} \right] \tag{23}$$

The remaining problem is that we do not actually know the true value of θ_j. To address this, we follow the same scheme as for MFII above and integrate across the interval $[\hat{\theta}_j - \delta, \hat{\theta}_j - \delta]$. Thus, we will calculate

$$\underset{i}{\text{argmax}} \left\{ \int_{\hat{\theta}-\delta}^{\hat{\theta}+\delta} \text{EKL}_i(\hat{\theta}_j; \theta_j) d\theta_j \right\}, \tag{24}$$

where again $\delta = z(\mathbb{I}(\hat{\theta}))^{-1/2}$ and z is a user specified z-value. This allows us to average across plausible values θ_j within z standard errors of our current estimate $\hat{\theta}$.

```
setSelection(ltm_cat)<-"KL"
select<-selectItem(ltm_cat)
select$next_item
```

[1] 3

As with the Fisher information criteria, this can be modified so that not all values of θ are considered equally plausible. Specifically, we can weight potential values of θ in Equation 24 by the height of the likelihood function and by the height of the (numerator of the) posterior. In the case of the likelihood function, this works out to be:

$$\underset{i}{\text{argmax}} \left\{ \int_{-\infty}^{\infty} \mathbb{L}(\theta_j | \mathbf{y}_j^{obs}) \text{EKL}_i(\hat{\theta}_j; \theta_j) \mathrm{d}\theta_j \right\}. \qquad (25)$$

We can also weight by the height of the likelihood function *and* the prior $\pi(\theta)$.

The primary difference between the various FI and KL approaches relates to the loss functions. Both favor items with large discrimination parameters (large in absolute terms). Both also favor items where the respondent is expected to have a relatively balanced chance of responding either "right" or "wrong." Kullback-Leibler information, however, is subtler in prioritizing items where a specific response will lead to a quick change in our estimate $\hat{\theta}_j$ so long as there is some decent probability of observing that response for plausible values of θ_j. Chang and Ying (1996), therefore, termed it "global information" and argue it will work better at initial phases of a CAT.

3.4.4 Explore on Your Own

Many of the mathematical operations discussed here come with their own specific functions in `catSurv` so that researchers can explore them on their own. For instance, the Fisher information for any item can be calculated using `fisherInf()`. All of the item selection routines also have specific functions so that researchers can manually calculate quantities like EPV (`expectedPV()`) or the expected observed information (`expectedObsInf()`).

3.5 Stopping Rules

The final choice researchers must make is when to stop asking questions. The `catSurv` package allows for four basic stopping rules, and you can set more than one stopping rule at the same time. There are also two "overrides" that will *prevent* a stopping rule from terminating the battery. For instance, the length override will make sure that the battery is *at least* of a certain length.

3.5.1 Stopping Thresholds

The simplest threshold is the length threshold, which will stop a survey once it reaches a specific length. We suggest always setting the length threshold to avoid asking the complete battery to some respondents.

```
setLengthThreshold(ltm_cat)<-4
checkStopRules(ltm_cat)
```

```
## [1] FALSE
```

A second option is to keep administering items until the standard error of the θ estimate falls below some threshold. This ensures that all respondents' positions on the latent scale have been measured with the same level of precision. This may be particularly desirable in situations where failure to accurately estimate a trait across its range can bias estimates (Bakker and Lelkes 2018). Here, for instance, we require that the current estimate for the standard error fall below 0.5 before stopping.

```
setSeThreshold(ltm_cat)<-.5
```

A third option is to ask questions until there are no more items remaining that fall above a specific threshold in terms of Fisher information. In essence, this criteria states that we should keep asking questions until there are none left that provide more information (`setInfoThreshold`).

The final stopping rule is to set a "gain threshold," where gain is measured in terms of posterior variance. Specifically, the gain is the difference between the current posterior standard deviation for θ and the square root of the expected posterior variance for each remaining item (`setGainThreshold`).

3.5.2 Stopping Overrides

While researchers can specify any or all of the stopping thresholds, in some cases they may wish to override a stopping rule. For instance, a researcher may wish to ensure that all respondents answer at *least* three questions even if no remaining items exceed the information threshold.

```
setLengthOverride(ltm_cat) <- 3
```

Finally, it may be desirable to keep asking questions even if, for instance, the length threshold has been exceeded. Specifically, `catSurv` allows for a gain threshold, where more questions will be asked so long as all remaining questions exceed a minimum threshold for expected improved precision. Specifically, questions will continue so long as $|se(\hat{\theta}) - \sqrt{EPV}| \geq q$ for some remaining item(s). With this final option, there is a risk that the algorithm may end up asking the complete battery. Researchers should always conduct simulation studies to ensure this doesn't happen before fielding a survey.

3.6 Binary Responses with Guessing

So far we have worked with a basic two-parameter IRT that included only the "difficulty" and "discrimination" parameters. This is sometimes referred to as a two-parameter logistic model (2PL). Another alternative in the literature is Birnbaum's three-parameter logistic (3PL) model shown in Equation 26 (Birnbaum 1968). This model was designed to allow for the fact that respondents may sometimes guess items at random and still get the question right.

$$\Pr_i(y_{ij} = 1|\theta_j) = c_i + (1 - c_i)\frac{\exp(a_i + b_i\theta_j)}{1 + \exp(a_i + b_i\theta_j)} \tag{26}$$

The only difference here is the introduction of the "guessing parameter," which indicates the probability that a respondent can get the answer correct (meaning, answer in a way we code '1') by responding at random.

To illustrate this, we return to our dataset of political knowledge questions and (for the sake of convenience) look only at the first 20 items. Note that in this case, we first fit the model directly in the ltm package and then pass the result to tpmCat() in order to set up the Cat object.

```
tpm_fit <- ltm::tpm(polknowMT[,1:20], start.val="random",
                max.guessing=0.1, control = list(optimizer = "nlminb"))
tpm_cat <- tpmCat(tpm_fit) # Passing an existing tpm model as an argument
```

You can again plot the IRF for the items. In this case, we also add a horizontal red line at the value of the guessing parameter (c_i) in Figure 16.

Although this model is fully implemented in catSurv, we have not used it ourselves. Based on our own simulations, we remain skeptical that the complications that come with it are worth the trouble. To begin, we advise researchers interested in the three-parameter model to scrutinize the model by examining the IRFs for all items and inspecting θ_j estimates relative to the standard 2PL. This is because the item parameter estimates can be wonky; it is possible to get extreme estimates that make no sense. And since convergence can be an issue, it is important not to ignore warnings.

Further, Samejima (1969) shows that it is easy to come up with examples where the 3PL model will result in multiple modes for the likelihood of θ_j. In

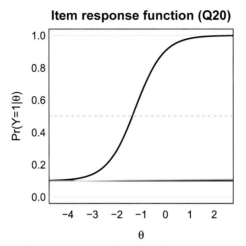

Figure 16 Example item response function for the three-parameter model

addition, unlike for the 2PL, the second derivative of the log-likelihood actually includes data that can result in unstable results (see section 3.2.3 in Baker and Kim (2004)). To reduce this instability, `catSurv` uses Fisher scoring for MLE and MAP, substituting in $-\mathbb{I}(\theta)$ for the denominator in Equation 11.[5] We recommend pretesting extensively and using the EAP estimation method if possible.

3.7 Technical Appendix

Let μ_θ and σ_θ be the prior mean and standard deviation respectively. We give the results for the 3PL model, and readers can just input $c_i = 0$ to get the results for the 2PL. Using this notation, the first derivative of the log-likelihood is given by:

$$\sum_{i=1}^{n} b_i \left(\frac{P_{ij} - c_i}{P_{ij}(1 - c_i)} \right)(y_{ij} - P_{ij}). \tag{27}$$

The first derivative of the log-posterior is:

$$\sum_{i=1}^{n} \left[b_i \left(\frac{P_{ij} - c_i}{P_{ij}(1 - c_i)} \right)(y_{ij} - P_{ij}) \right] - \left(\frac{\theta_j - \mu_\theta}{\sigma_\theta^2} \right). \tag{28}$$

The second derivative of the log-likelihood is:

$$-\sum_{i=1}^{n} b_i^2 \left(\frac{P_{ij} - c_i}{1 - c_i} \right)^2 \frac{Q_{ij}}{P_{ij}}. \tag{29}$$

---

[5] We also note that this means that MEI item selection for this model is actually based on the "expected" Fisher information rather than the expected observed information.

The second derivative of the log-posterior is:

$$-\sum_{i=1}^{n}\left[b_i^2\left(\frac{P_{ij}-c_i}{1-c_i}\right)^2\frac{Q_{ij}}{P_{ij}}\right]-\frac{1}{\sigma_\theta^2}. \tag{30}$$

Note that this last equation is actually the expected value of the second derivative for the 3PL model rather than the observed information. As noted, the observed and Fisher information are identical for the 2PL model.

3.7.1 Weighted Maximum Likelihood Estimation

The WLE estimate is calculated by finding the root of Equation 31 such that,

$$W(\theta_j) = \mathbb{L}(\theta_j|\mathbf{y}_j^{\text{obs}}) + \frac{B(\theta_j)}{2\mathbb{I}(\theta_j)} = 0 \tag{31}$$

where

$$B(\theta_j) = \sum_i \frac{P'_{ij}P''_{ij}}{P_{ij}Q_{ij}}.$$

In this case, P_{ij} and Q_{ij} are as defined above, and

$$P'_{ij} = b_i(1-c_i)\frac{\exp(a_i+b_i\theta_j)}{(1+\exp(a_i+b_i\theta_j))^2}$$

and,

$$P''_{ij} = b^2\exp(a_i+b_i\theta_j)(1-\exp(a_i+b_i\theta_j))\frac{(1-c)}{(1+\exp(a_i+b_i\theta_j))^3}.$$

4 CAT for Polytomous Outcomes

The previous sections discussed AIs for binary outcomes. However, most survey batteries feature more than two response options. When this is the case, CAT requires a polytomous IRT model (Dodd, De Ayala, and Koch 1995). This section presents two models for polytomous outcomes: the graded response model (GRM) and the generalized partial credit model (GPCM).

This section introduces these models and discusses when and how to adjust the CAT algorithm to handle categorical responses. There are some slightly different mathematical results, mostly relating to how the likelihood is defined. Therefore, we focus primarily on the GRM and GPCM themselves and only discuss the more technical aspects of the CAT procedures where they must be adjusted significantly from the previous presentation. For the most part, the process is the same as discussed in Sections 2 and 3. Indeed, researchers can use the same basic workhorse functions from `catSurv` and almost all of the options and procedures are unchanged.

4.1 Graded Response Model (GRM)

The GRM is appropriate when the response options are assumed to be ordered and the order is known in advance (Baker and Kim 2004; Samejima 1969). For example, a Likert scale is a common form of question where respondents may choose from options ranging from "agree strongly" to "disagree strongly."

To demonstrate the GRM, we will use the Need for Cognition (NFC) personality battery originally proposed to measure, "the tendency for an individual to engage in and enjoy thinking" (Cacioppo and Petty 1982, p. 116). The items in this battery use a five-point Likert scale with the options agree strongly, agree somewhat, neither agree nor disagree, disagree somewhat, disagree strongly. Run ?nfc for additional information about this battery and question wording. As noted in Section 1, this adaptive battery was included on the 2016 ANES Pilot study.

4.1.1 Calculating Probabilities

Just as with the binary model, the first piece of information needed is the item response function (IRF). The IRF is the conditional probability that a respondent provides a specific answer to a survey item given their position on the latent scale of interest in Figure 17.

To start, assume that there are two or more response categories, $k \in [1, C_i]$, for each item $i \in [1, n]$. Note that the index C_i allows for different numbers of response categories for different question items. Our task is now to calculate $P_{ij,k} = \text{Pr}_{ik}(y_{ij} = k|\theta_j)$, the probability of respondent j answering category k for item i. This probability cannot be calculated directly. Instead, we first calculate a *cumulative* probability of answering category k *or lower*:

$$P^*_{ij,k} = \text{Pr}_{ik}(y_{ij} \leq k|\theta_j) = \frac{\exp(\kappa_{ik} - b_i\theta_j)}{1 + \exp(\kappa_{ik} - b_i\theta_j)}. \tag{32}$$

For each item i there is now a *vector* of threshold parameters defined as $\kappa_i = (\kappa_{i0}, \kappa_{i1}, \ldots, \kappa_{iC_i})$, with $\kappa_{i0} < \kappa_{i1} \leq \ldots < \kappa_{iC_i}$. The first and last threshold parameters are not estimated, but rather, are assumed to be $\kappa_{i0} = -\infty$ and $\kappa_{iC_i} = \infty$, respectively. This leaves $C_i - 1$ threshold parameters to estimate. These threshold parameters are analogous to the difficulty parameter of the binary model. In addition, each item is associated with a discrimination parameter b_i, which indicates how well item i corresponds to the underlying trait.

So the cumulative probability that respondent j for item i gives answer k or lower is $P^*_{ij,k}$. Since these are cumulative probabilities, note that $P^*_{ij,C_i} = 1$. However, this is not actually the quantity of interest. We are ultimately interested in the probability a respondent provides response k. But finding this

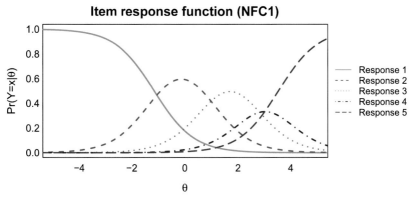

Figure 17 Example item response function for Need for Cognition item 1

probability is as simple as subtracting the cumulative probability that the respondent provided answer $k - 1$ from the cumulative probability that the respondent provided answer k:

$$\Pr_{ik}(y_{ij} = k|\theta_j) = P_{ij,k} = P^*_{ij,k} - P^*_{ij,k-1}. \tag{33}$$

To make this more concrete, consider a sample where we have responses to the full NFC inventory. Using this data, we estimate the item parameters and store them in a Cat object using the grmCat() function.

```
data("nfc")
nfc_cat <- grmCat(nfc, quadraturePoints = 100)
```

Each item has five response options, so four threshold parameters and a discrimination parameter are estimated for each item. For example, the estimated parameters for the first question item are:

```
nfc_cat@difficulty[[1]]
```

```
## [1] -1.543414  1.203181  3.369304  4.748987
```

```
nfc_cat@discrimination[1]
```

```
##      NFC1
## 1.341952
```

The function probability() will calculate $P^*_{ij,k}$, or the *cumulative* probabilities as shown in Equation 32, and return a vector of values. To calculate $P_{ij,k}$, the probabilities associated with answering each of the five response options, simply take the difference between lagged categories with the diff() function.

```
p_star <- probability(nfc_cat, theta = 0, item = 1)
p_star # cumulative probabilities
```

```
## [1] 0.0000000 0.1760396 0.7690902 0.9667313 0.9914139
## [6] 1.0000000
```

```
p <- diff(p_star)
p # category probabilities
```

```
## [1] 0.176039568 0.593050672 0.197641063 0.024682592
## [5] 0.008586105
```

The estimated category probabilities for a respondent with a true position at 0 on the latent trait is highest for the second response option of "disagree somewhat." You can also visualize this by plotting the item response function for the first item in Figure 17.

```
plot(nfc_cat, item = 1, plotType = "IRF", xlim = c(-5, 5))
```

Just as before, the horizontal axis represents a respondent's position in the latent space. The IRF is the probability of observing each response as a function of θ_j (thus there are five curves).

As explained in Section 2, the first item's discrimination parameter is constrained to be positive. In this case, the first item is, "I really enjoy a task that involves coming up with new solutions to problems." The NFC response options are coded as '1' = agree strongly, '2' = agree somewhat, ..., '5' = disagree strongly. Since "larger" response options actually indicate "less" of the latent trait for the first item, the $\hat{\theta}_j$ estimates should be interpreted as follows: large, positive positions on the latent trait actually indicate less NFC; large, negative values indicate more NFC. For a more intuitive interpretation, users can reverse code the final estimates or change the first item in the calibration data so that higher values indicate "more" of the latent trait.

To get an intuition for the role of the item parameters, we plot and compare the IRF for multiple items in Figure 18 here. NFC4 and NFC31 have large discrimination parameters (1.50 and -1.32) compared to NFC12 (0.599). Visually, these differences manifest in the steepness of the response curves.

The sign of the discrimination parameter is also visually apparent. Items NFC4 and NFC31 have positive and negative discrimination parameters, respectively. This difference in sign indicates a "flip" in how the response options relate to the latent trait. Plotting an item characteristic curve (ICC) is

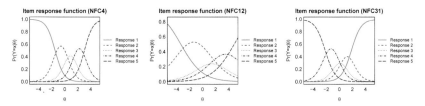

Figure 18 Item response functions for three items

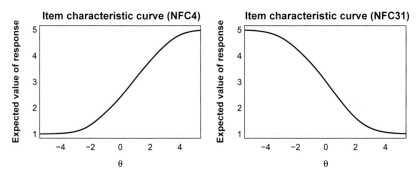

Figure 19 Item response functions for two items

another way to visualize item information, shown in Figure 19. The ICC calculates the expected value of the response across values of the latent trait on the x-axis.[6]

```
par(mfrow = c(1, 2))
plot(nfc_cat, item = 2, plotType = "ICC", xlim = c(-5, 5))
plot(nfc_cat, item = 13, plotType = "ICC", xlim = c(-5, 5))
```

4.1.2 Likelihood

The likelihood of observing person j's response profile $\mathbf{y}_j^{\text{obs}}$ is the joint probability of observing each recorded response to the questions asked:

$$\mathbb{L}(\theta_j|\mathbf{y}_j) = \prod_{i=1}^{n}\prod_{k=1}^{C_i} P_{ij,k}^{I(y_{ij}=k)} = \exp\left[\sum_{i=1}^{n}\sum_{k=1}^{C_i}\log\left(P_{ij,k}^{I(y_{ij}=k)}\right)\right], \tag{34}$$

where $I(.)$ is the usual indicator function that evaluates to 1 when the equality holds and evaluates to zero otherwise.

Consider a scenario in which a respondent has answered '2', '1', and '5' to items 2, 6, and 14, respectively. Assigning these answers in the Cat object and plotting the likelihood for different values of θ gives the likelihood function. The shape of the likelihood in Figure 20 indicates that this response profile

---

[6] In the binary case, the IRF and ICC are equivalent.

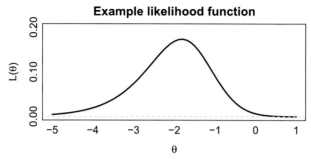

Figure 20 Likelihood function for a respondent who has answered three questions

is most likely for a respondent whose position is around $\theta = -2$ (indicating a high level of NFC).

```
ans_profile <- rep(NA, ncol(nfc)) # Vector of missing responses
ans_profile[c(2, 6, 14)] <- c(2, 1, 5) # Answers for the chosen items
setAnswers(nfc_cat) <- ans_profile # Storing these answers in the Cat object
```

4.1.3 Estimating the Respondents' Locations

Sections 2 and 3 detailed four estimation routines to complete the first step in the CAT algorithm – estimating a respondent's current position on the latent trait. These methods are not model specific, meaning that while the likelihood and probability equations change between models, the statistical routines used in executing the CAT algorithm do not. Therefore, we will refer readers to those sections for a detailed explanation of the latent trait estimation routines.

With this in mind, let's return to our hypothetical respondent. In order to estimate their position on the latent trait, first indicate "EAP" as the estimation routine and specify a prior. Then, you can estimate the respondent's position on the latent trait, $\hat{\theta}_j$, and the standard error of this estimate by calling the estimateTheta() and estimateSE() functions.

```
setEstimation(nfc_cat) <- "EAP" # set estimation routine
setPriorName(nfc_cat) <- "NORMAL" # specify prior
setPriorParams(nfc_cat) <- c(0,1.5) # specify prior parameters, N(0,1)
estimateTheta(nfc_cat)
```

```
## [1] -1.531141
```

```
estimateSE(nfc_cat)
```

```
## [1] 0.6913234
```

4.1.4 Item Selection and Stopping Rules

Sections 2 and 3 also detailed nine item selection routines. For the most part, item selection routines are not model specific. Although the details of the math change (since the likelihoods are different), the basic ideas are the same. We again refer readers to those sections for a more detailed discussion. Still, there are a few differences worth considering.

Recall that $P_{ij,k} = P^*_{ij,k} - P^*_{ij,k-1}$. Further, let $Q^*_{ij,k} = 1 - P^*_{ij,k}$, $w_{ij,k-1} = P^*_{ij,k-1} Q^*_{ij,k-1}$, and $w_{ij,k} = P^*_{ij,k} Q^*_{ij,k}$. For the graded response model, the log-likelihood is

$$\log \mathbb{L}(\theta_j | \mathbf{y}^{obs}_j) \equiv \lambda(\theta_j | \mathbf{y}^{obs}_j) = \left[\sum_{i=1}^{n} \sum_{k=1}^{C_i} I(y_{ij} = k) \log \left(P_{ij,k} \right) \right].$$

The first derivative of the log-likelihood is then

$$\frac{\mathrm{d}\lambda}{\mathrm{d}\theta_j} = \sum_{i=1}^{n} \sum_{k=1}^{C_i} I(y_{ij} = k) \left[-b_i \left(\frac{w_{ij,k} - w_{ij,k-1}}{P_{ij,k}} \right) \right],$$

and the second derivative is

$$\frac{\mathrm{d}^2\lambda}{\mathrm{d}\theta_j^2} = \sum_{i=1}^{n} -b_i^2 \sum_{k=1}^{C_i} I(y_{ij} = k) \left[\frac{-w_{ij,k-1}(Q^*_{ij,k-1} - P^*_{ij,k-1}) + w_{ij,k}(Q^*_{ij,k} - P^*_{ij,k})}{P_{ij,k}} - \frac{(w_{ij,k} - w_{ij,k-1})^2}{P_{ij,k}^2} \right].$$

One notable difference is that the observed information now actually includes the data via the indicator function. (Recall that the observed information $J(\theta_j | \mathbf{y}^{obs}_j) = -\mathrm{d}^2\lambda/\mathrm{d}\theta_j^2$.) To find the Fisher information, we need to take the expectation, $\mathbb{E}_y \left(J(\theta_j | \mathbf{y}^{obs}_j) \right)$, which is:

$$\mathbb{I}(\theta_j) = \sum_{i=1}^{n} \sum_{k=1}^{C_i} b_i^2 \frac{(w_{ij,k} - w_{ij,k-1})^2}{P^*_{ij,k} - P^*_{ij,k-1}}.$$

See chapter 8.3 in Baker and Kim (2004) for a detailed explanation.

The portion associated with each item i is then:

$$\mathbb{I}_i(\theta_j) = \sum_{k=1}^{C_i} b_i^2 \frac{(w_{ij,k} - w_{ij,k-1})^2}{P^*_{ij,k} - P^*_{ij,k-1}}.$$

Intuitively, this says that the information will be higher for items with large discrimination parameters and where the respondent has a high probability of answering in multiple response categories. With these, the standard FI selection criteria are the same as in Section 3 when you substitute in the appropriate formula for $\mathbb{I}_i(\theta_j)$ or $J(\theta_j | \mathbf{y}^{obs}_j)$ associated with the GRM.

The functions needed to do item selection remain unchanged once the Cat object is set up correctly. For example, let's use the maximum posterior weighted information method by using the setSelection() function and assigning "MPWI." The MPWI for each unasked item is returned as a data frame, where each row includes the item index, a unique item identifier, and the MPWI estimate. Note that since our hypothetical respondent answered items 2, 6, and 14, the algorithm excludes these items from the procedure of selecting the next question. Of the remaining unasked items, item 10 (NFC23) is the optimal item to ask this respondent next.

```
setSelection(nfc_cat) <- "MPWI"
select <- selectItem(nfc_cat)
head(select$estimates, 5) # data frame of estimates for unasked items

##    q_number q_name        MPWI
## 1         1   NFC1 0.016684212
## 2         3  NFC10 0.019795918
## 3         4  NFC12 0.004259418
## 4         5  NFC15 0.024962647
## 5         7  NFC19 0.020561291

select$next_item # index of selected item

## [1] 10

select$next_item_name # name of selected item

## [1] "NFC23"
```

The remaining criteria change only modestly to account for the multiple categories. The MEPV criteria, for instance, becomes:

$$\operatorname*{argmin}_{i}\left\{\sum_{k=1}^{C_i} \underbrace{\Pr(y^*_{ij} = k)|\hat{\theta}_j)}_{\text{Prob. } y^*_{ij}=k} \overbrace{\mathbb{V}\mathrm{ar}(\theta|y^*_{ij} = k, \mathbf{y}^{\mathrm{obs}}_j)}^{\text{Posterior variance if } y^*_{ij}=k}\right\}.$$

Likewise, the core of the Kullback-Leibler selection method becomes:

$$\mathrm{EKL}_i(\hat{\theta}_j; \theta_j) = \sum_{k=1}^{C_i} \underbrace{\Pr_i(y^*_{ij} = k)|\hat{\theta}_j)}_{\text{Prob. } y^*_{ij}=k} \log \overbrace{\frac{\Pr_i(y^*_{ij} = k|\theta_j)}{\Pr_i(y^*_{ij} = k|\hat{\theta}_j)}}^{\text{Information gain if } y^*_{ij}=k}.$$

The final step in this process, checking stopping rules, is again unmodified. Here we set the stopping rule to be a battery of length three and check if this condition is met.

```
setLengthThreshold(nfc_cat) <- 3 # Set the threshold
checkStopRules(nfc_cat) # Check
## [1] TRUE
```

4.2 Generalized Partial Credit Model (GPCM)

Another option for survey batteries that feature more than two response options is the Generalized Partial Credit Model (GPCM) (Muraki 1992; Muraki and Muraki 2016). Like the GRM, the GPCM is appropriate for successively ordered response options. But the GPCM is also appropriate when the exact ordering of options is not known in advance.

Consider polytomous data where the answer can be considered as either "right" or "wrong." For example, political scientists often want to know respondents' levels of political knowledge, and a question asked to measure this latent trait is, "Who is the Chief Justice of the US Supreme Court?" Response options from a May 2013 administration of this political knowledge battery were John Roberts, Antonin Scalia, Mitt Romney, and Hillary Clinton. While there are four response options, there are three incorrect options and one correct option. So we could actually think of these data as binary – the respondent provides either a correct or an incorrect answer.

However, consider a respondent who answered Hillary Clinton and a respondent who answered Antonin Scalia. It seems that while the first respondent essentially knows nothing about the Supreme Court, the second respondent was in some ways "less wrong" by at least recognizing Antonin Scalia as a Supreme Court Justice. The GPCM uses this information – the "steps" a respondent takes toward the correct answer – and allows for *partial credit* in the scoring of answers.

For the GPCM model, our presentation follows Muraki (1992). The probability of respondent j choosing response option k for item i is:

$$\Pr_{ik}(y_{ij} = k | \theta_j) = \frac{\exp(\sum_{t=1}^{k} \alpha_i(\theta_j - \delta_{it}))}{\sum_{r=1}^{C_i} \exp(\sum_{t=1}^{r} \alpha_i(\theta_j - \delta_{it}))}, \tag{35}$$

where θ_j is respondent j's position on the latent trait, α_i is the discrimination parameter for item i, and δ_{ik} is the threshold parameter for item i for category k, with $k \in [1, C_i]$. There are $C_i - 1$ threshold parameters for item i. These parameters describe the relationship between adjacent response options, thus we need only $C_i - 1$ parameters to do so.

One key difference in the GRM and GPCM is the interpretation of the difficulty or threshold parameters. Unlike the GRM, the GPCM threshold parameters are not constrained to be ordered and can take on any real value.

The difficulty parameters for the GPCM are not cumulative like with the GRM, but instead only dictate the probability of a respondent answering adjacent response options. Specifically, the threshold parameters tell us at what point on the latent trait the kth response option is equally likely as response option $k + 1$. That is, the threshold parameter represents the point $\theta_j = \delta_{ik}$ at which $\Pr_{ik}(y_{ij} = k|\theta_j) = \Pr_{i,k+1}(y_{ij} = k + 1|\theta_j)$.

To illustrate this, we fit a GPCM to five political knowledge questions asked on The American Panel Survey (see ?polknowOrdered for more information). This example works because we know not only whether the respondent was right or wrong, but which specific answer they chose. We can visualize the IRF for three different items to get some intuition for the GPCM item parameters. First, create a Cat object using the gpcmCat() function, which estimates item parameters for the GPCM model from our sample data. Note that in the sample data, increasing values mean more "partial credit" is assigned with 5 always indicating the correct option and 1 always indicating the "Don't Know" option. This may not be the case for other similar surveys.

```
data("polknowOrdered")
polknow_cat <- gpcmCat(polknowOrdered[,c("Q1","Q4","Q6","Q7","Q8")])
```

Next, use the plot() function to plot IRFs for questions 1, 4, and 7. Interpretation of the discrimination parameters is no different for the GPCM and GRM. We see in Figure 21 that the curves for question 1 are much steeper than those of question 4, reflected numerically in the item parameter estimates. Also, both α_1 and α_4 are positive, demonstrating that higher response options are associated with more political knowledge (larger values of the latent trait).

```
polknow_cat@discrimination[c("Q1", "Q4")]

##         Q1         Q4
## 0.9258931 0.2515835
```

```
par(mfrow = c(1, 3))
plot(polknow_cat, item = 1, plotType = "IRF", xlim = c(-5, 5))
plot(polknow_cat, item = 2, plotType = "IRF", xlim = c(-5, 5))
plot(polknow_cat, item = 4, plotType = "IRF", xlim = c(-5, 5))
```

You can also visualize the difficulty parameters on the plot by examining where the lines for adjacent response options intersect. Returning again to Figure 21, for item 7, answering response '2' or response '3' is equally likely at $\theta_j = -2.48$. We can visualize this on the plot by seeing that the blue and pink lines do indeed intersect around $\theta_j = -2.5$.

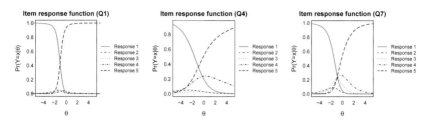

Figure 21 Item response functions for three items

```
polknow_cat@difficulty[["Q7"]][2]
```

```
## [1] -2.485156
```

Note that, overall, these IRFs show that either answering "don't know" or getting the answer correct are always the most probable responses (these are responses '1' and '5' in all cases). For example, when a respondent is most likely to choose option '4' to item 7 is when θ_j is large. However, for these same values of θ, respondents are still *most* likely to get the question right (response 5) since the dashed red line is highest. In fact, it is *always* most probable for respondents with (roughly) $\theta_j > -1$ to get the question right and respondents with $\theta_j < -1$ to answer that they do not know.

This observation makes sense in light of the data. The political knowledge questions are fairly easy, factual questions, and the marginal frequencies of response options '2', '3', and '4' are low across the board. For numerical reasons, this can actually be problematic. Since so few respondents actually chose those response options, the model parameters might be poorly calibrated. We advise proceeding with caution when using the GPCM, especially when frequencies for certain response options are very low.

Turning back to the broader CAT algorithm, the next steps are the same as before. As with the GRM model, the procedure and options for estimating respondents' positions on the latent trait and selecting items to administer for the GPCM are no different than the procedure for the binary model outlined in Section 3.

Finally, after the researcher specifies their preferences for the estimation and item selection steps, selecting the best item to administer to a respondent just takes the selectItem() function. Having administered no items, here we use selectItem() to choose the first item to administer to the respondents. We see that administering the fourth question is most likely to decrease our uncertainty about respondents' positions on the latent trait.

```
setEstimation(polknow_cat) <- "EAP"
setPriorName(polknow_cat) <- "NORMAL"
```

```
setPriorParams(polknow_cat) <- c(0,1)
setSelection(polknow_cat) <- "EPV"
selectItem(polknow_cat)$next_item_name
```

[1] "Q7"

As with the GRM, the main difference here is in how the derivatives and information terms are defined. Breaking up the terms in Equation 35, let $f = \exp(\sum_{t=1}^{k} \alpha_i(\theta_j - \delta_{it}))$ and $g = \sum_{r=1}^{C_i} \exp(\sum_{t=1}^{r} \alpha_i(\theta_j - \delta_{it}))$. Their derivatives are simply $f' = \exp(\sum_{t=1}^{k} \alpha_i(\theta_j - \delta_{it})) \cdot \alpha_i \cdot k$, $f'' = \exp(\sum_{t=1}^{k} \alpha_i(\theta_j - \delta_{it})) \cdot \alpha_i^2 \cdot k^2$, $g' = \sum_{r=1}^{C_i} [\exp(\sum_{t=1}^{r} \alpha_i(\theta_j - \delta_{it})) \cdot \alpha_i \cdot \sum_{t=1}^{r} 1]$, and $g'' = \sum_{r=1}^{C_i} [\exp(\sum_{t=1}^{r} \alpha_i(\theta_j - \delta_{it})) \cdot \alpha_i^2 \cdot (\sum_{t=1}^{r} 1)^2]$. With these quantities, we can state the first and second derivatives of $P_{ij,k}$ as:

$$P'_{ij,k} = \frac{g \cdot f' - g' \cdot f}{g^2}$$

and

$$P''_{ij,k} = \frac{(g^2)(f''g - g''f) - (2g'g)(f'g - g'f)}{g^4}.$$

The log likelihood is then:

$$\lambda(\theta_j | \mathbf{y}_j^{obs}) \equiv \log L(\theta_j | \mathbf{y}_j^{obs}) = \sum_{i=1}^{n} \sum_{k=1}^{C_i} I(y_{jk} = k) \log\left(P_{ij,k}\right).$$

The first derivative of the log-likelihood is then:

$$\frac{d\lambda}{d\theta_j} = \sum_{i=1}^{n} \sum_{k=1}^{C_i} I(y_{jk} = k)\left(\frac{P'_{ij,k}}{P_{ij,k}}\right),$$

and the second derivative is

$$\frac{d^2\lambda}{d\theta_j^2} = -\sum_{i=1}^{n} \sum_{k=1}^{C_i} I(y_{jk} = k)\left(\frac{P'^2_{ij,k}}{P^2_{ij,k}} - \frac{P''_{ij,k}}{P_{ij,k}}\right).$$

The observed information for item i, assuming the answer was response option k, is:

$$\frac{P'^2_{ij,k}}{P^2_{ij,k}} - \frac{P''_{ij,k}}{P_{ij,k}}.$$

Taking the expectation, the component of the Fisher information for item i is:

$$\mathbb{I}_i(\theta) = \sum_{k=1}^{C_i} \frac{P'^2_{ij,k}}{P_{ij,k}} - P''_{ij,k}.$$

5 Evaluating Adaptive Inventories

To this point, this Element has detailed different response models, item selection routines, stopping rules, and other options for AIs. Given this somewhat dizzying array of options, how should researchers choose among them? More fundamentally, how can we evaluate whether an adaptive battery is "good" or if using CAT will help or hinder our research goals?

In Section 5, we provide several different criteria that researchers may wish to use to assess a single battery or to compare their options.

(1) Researchers may want to evaluate the speed of each algorithm.
(2) Researchers can use answers from real-world respondents to assess the accuracy and efficiency of CAT estimates relative to alternative approaches (including fixed batteries).
(3) Researchers can perform simulations to assess battery performance in a context where we *know* what the true estimates of θ_j should be for each respondent.

In this section, we explain how to evaluate a proposed battery in all three ways. To motivate this task, we will return to the GRM battery measuring need for cognition (NFC) discussed in Section 4. For the sake of exposition, assume our goal is to develop a two-item adaptive inventory to replace the two-item fixed battery traditionally included on the American National Election Study. The two items that have historically been included on the ANES (NFC1 and NFC4) were chosen because they loaded strongly on the latent construct in Cacioppo and Petty's (1982) factor analysis (Bizer et al. 2000).

Two items is short for an adaptive battery. We typically recommend that there be at least three items to really leverage the method's advantages. Still, as we will show, we can get modest improvements over this fixed battery even with two items. However, at the end of this section, we present results from a more intensive examination of a four-item adaptive battery of neuroticism.

To get things started, we will create a GRM Cat object using the `nfc` dataset included in the `catSurv` package.

```
data(nfc)
nfc_cat <- grmCat(nfc, quadraturePoints = 100)
```

We can then estimate respondents' positions on the latent trait using the ANES two-item fixed battery. This will be our baseline.

```
fixed_items <- c("NFC1", "NFC4") # Column names of fixed battery

# keep data only for "fixed" battery
```

```
respondents_fixed <- nfc
respondents_fixed[,-which(colnames(nfc) %in% fixed_items)] <- NA

# generate fixed battery estimates
fixed_thetas <- estimateThetas(catObj = nfc_cat,
                               responses = respondents_fixed)
```

Next, we set up two AIs, one with the MFI item selection routine and the other with MEPV, that we will use as examples throughout this section. Both AIs have a length threshold of two items. We leave the rest of the CAT options at their default values.

```
setLengthThreshold(nfc_cat)<-2 # Stop after two questions
nfc_cat_MFI<-nfc_cat_EPV<-nfc_cat # Make duplicates of original battery

# Set different item selections
setSelection(nfc_cat_MFI)<-"MFI"
setSelection(nfc_cat_EPV)<-"EPV"
```

Which of these selection routines is "best," and are either of them better than the traditional fixed battery? The rest of this section attempts to answer these questions.

5.1 Item Selection Speed

For most small batteries (with fewer than 40 questions), catSurv is sufficiently fast and all methods have practically equivalent speed. However, there may be exceptions to this rule, and there are even larger batteries where speed may come into play. Here we use the microbenchmark package to test the relative speed of two models.[7]

microbenchmark runs selectItem 100 times and reports back the execution time in milliseconds (1 millisecond = 0.001 second).

```
speedTest<-microbenchmark::microbenchmark(selectItem(nfc_cat_MFI),
                                          selectItem(nfc_cat_EPV),
                                          times=100)
summary(speedTest, unit="ms")[,c("min", "mean", "median", "max")]

##         min       mean     median        max
## 1 0.406502 0.4943517  0.4778625  0.841549
## 2 1.011677 1.1733781  1.1365885  1.620896
```

---

[7] These calculations were performed on a MacBook Pro with a 1.4 GHz Quad-Core Intel processor running macOS Catalina version 10.15.6.

Table 2 Completion times in milliseconds

Criteria	25th %	Mean	Median	75th %
MFI	0.408	0.422	0.411	0.418
MPWI	0.529	0.549	0.538	0.550
MEI	0.744	0.763	0.750	0.757
PKL	0.596	0.622	0.603	0.610
EPV	1.016	1.054	1.026	1.050

These results show that the median time for selecting items using the MFI criteria was 0.478 milliseconds or 4.78×10^{-4} seconds. Meanwhile, the median time using the EPV criteria was 1.137 milliseconds. We can see that the although MFI is obviously faster, both methods execute in far less than 0.01 seconds, making this distinction irrelevant.

Generalizing this approach, in Table 2 we compare several more of the item selection routines we covered earlier. We exclude routines that rely entirely on the likelihood, which is not defined for selecting the first item. The results in Table 2 show that although there are some noticeable differences, all of these routines execute in less than 0.01 seconds, indicating that speed is not a practical concern in this case. More broadly, in our experience, the greatest slowdown for CAT comes not from execution speed but from network lag.

5.2 Performance Based on Final Estimates

Another way to evaluate competing CAT batteries is to compare how accurately they recover respondents' "true" positions on the latent trait. While an attractive idea, evaluating alternatives based on performance is tricky in practice.

We have developed two approaches to evaluate battery performance for accuracy. First, we use real responses to the *complete* battery from actual survey respondents. This has the advantage that responses reflect the kinds of real-world patterns we might expect to see in the field. The disadvantage is that we can never really be sure that we know the "true" position of respondents on the latent trait.

Second, we present pure simulation methods where the true θ_j parameters are known and we simulate response profiles from the IRT model. This approach allows us to truly evaluate how well each method approximates respondents' underlying positions. However, the simulated profiles tend to be too "neat" and do not deviate from the model as they would in real-world settings. Obviously, neither approach is perfect, so we recommend testing your batteries both ways.

Before providing details, however, we outline our general strategy. Recall from Section 3 that for respondent j we denote her true position on the latent trait as θ_j and her complete set of responses to the battery as $\mathbf{y_j}$. Let $\mathcal{B}$ be the complete set of n items and $\mathcal{S}_j \subset \mathcal{B}$ be the subset of items as selected by CAT model $\mathcal{M}$. $\mathcal{M}$ denotes parameter estimation methods, item selection routines, stopping rules, and all of the other choices that go into setting up a Cat object.

With this notation, we can define a loss function $\mathcal{L}_j(\mathcal{S}_j|\mathcal{M}, \theta_j, \mathbf{y}_j)$, which represents the loss in terms of accuracy or efficiency from using the subset of items $\mathcal{S}_j$ as selected for that respondent by CAT model $\mathcal{M}$. For some population of respondents, we can then calculate the collective loss as $\mathcal{L}(\mathcal{S}|\mathcal{M}, \theta, \mathbf{Y})$. In words, this means that we want to look at respondents imagining we know all of the responses they would give to the *complete* battery. Then we apply model $\mathcal{M}$ using those responses and compare the estimate it provides ($\hat{\theta}_j$) to the "true" value (θ_j). We then do this for multiple models, creating a clean comparison where θ and $\mathbf{Y}$ are fixed.

The difficulty with real-world data is that we have $\mathbf{Y}$, but we have to guess at θ. We do this by assuming that the "best" estimate would be generated using responses to the complete battery (although this is not necessarily the case). Thus, we are in essence comparing $\hat{\theta}_j$ as estimated using the complete response set to the $\hat{\theta}_j$ as estimated using only the items chosen by model $\mathcal{M}$.

The problem with simulated data is that we have to decide how to generate θ and $\mathbf{Y}$. In our case, we simulate the response sets to all items based on the assumed model $\Pr_i(y_{ij} = k|\theta_j)$. This is probably too strong an assumption and biases the results in favor of the CAT algorithms. We generate θ uniformly along a fixed interval. This allows us to better understand model performance for a range of θ_j values, but may oversupply simulated respondents at extreme (or unusual) positions.

A final challenge is determining a baseline. Reduced batteries will never approximate a full battery perfectly. And even the complete battery will not provide perfect estimates for θ_j in all cases. This is especially true for "extreme" individuals with θ_j values far from zero. So, if perfection is unlikely, how do we know if our results are good or bad?

To solve this problem, we introduce two additional models that can give us a range of good and bad outcomes. As a worst-case scenario, we look at the performance of a battery with random item selection. That is, for each respondent, we select items at random until it reaches the stopping threshold. Any good adaptive battery (of the same length) should outperform random selection.

```
nfc_cat_RANDOM<-nfc_cat # Setting up a random baseline CAT
setSelection(nfc_cat_RANDOM)<-"RANDOM"
```

We also created an "oracle" model that we can use for short batteries to establish an upper bound for performance. If the reduced battery is of length s, the oracle model actually estimates $\hat{\theta}_j$ for all $\binom{n}{s}$ reduced batteries and selects the one that would result in the smallest absolute error $|\hat{\theta}_j - \theta_j|$. It does this for each respondent separately, and therefore represents the maximum level of accuracy.

For batteries longer than five questions, the oracle task can become computationally intractable. Moreover, in our experience, the oracle quickly converges to perfection at about $s = 5$ so long as there is a reasonably sized battery to choose from. This means that we can often approximate the oracle results just by assuming zero error for AIs of six or longer. Alternatively, we provide an option to approximate the oracle using 1,000 randomly selected question combinations and choosing the best reduced battery from this set. This provides a reasonable approximation to the oracle battery with significantly lower computational overhead.

5.2.1 Simulations from Real World Data

First, we evaluate the performance of the adaptive battery relative to the estimates we would get by administering the complete battery to all respondents. The easiest way to do this is with the dataset originally used to calibrate the CAT object, although you could also "hold out" a sample for this purpose.

To illustrate, we estimate $\hat{\theta}_j$ based on the complete response set of the first 500 respondents in our sample. We evaluate each alternative as if these estimates are correct. In practice, researchers will want to use a larger sample.

```
# Estimating the final theta estimates for first 500 respondents
responses<-nfc[1:500,]
complete_estimates<-estimateThetas(catObj=nfc_cat,
                              responses=responses)
```

The next step is to determine how well the various AIs do in approximating these final estimates. To do this, we simply allow the algorithm to choose a question for each respondent in the dataset and then "record" their response. Based on that response, the algorithm then selects the next item and the answer is "recorded." This is repeated until the stopping rule is reached and the final $\hat{\theta}_j$ estimate from this procedure is returned. While this may seem cumbersome, all of these steps can be executed using the `simulateThetas()` function that takes in as arguments a list of Cat objects of interest and the set of responses the algorithms should draw from. Here, we compare the MFI to the MEPV item selection routines. At the same time, we can also generate random estimates.

```
set.seed(1) # Set random seed to make random results replicate
theta_ests_real<-simulateThetas(catObjs=list(MFI=nfc_cat_MFI,
                                              EPV=nfc_cat_EPV,
                                              Random=nfc_cat_RANDOM),
                                responses=responses)
colnames(theta_ests_real) <- c("MFI", "EPV", "Random")
head(theta_ests_real, 4)
```

```
##            MFI         EPV        Random
## 1  -0.8211727  -0.8211727  -0.4634051
## 2   0.2877666   0.2877666   0.1986469
## 3   1.3263284   1.3263284   0.9305885
## 4  -0.2401981  -0.2401981   1.0066654
```

Here we can see the estimates generated for the first four respondents using only the two-item battery.

We can also create an oracle battery to provide a baseline for the best possible performance. Note that even for 500 respondents and two items, this takes some time to execute.

```
oracleEstimates<-oracle(catObj = nfc_cat, # Original battery
                        theta = complete_estimates, # True theta values
                        responses = responses) # Response profiles
theta_ests_real$oracle<-oracleEstimates$theta_est
```

Finally, we can add in the estimates from the fixed battery:

```
theta_ests_real$fixed<-fixed_thetas[1:500]
```

The next step is to compare the models in terms of accuracy. For instance, the root mean squared error (RMSE) for the algorithm can be calculated as:

$$\text{RMSE} = \sqrt{\frac{(\hat{\theta}_j - \theta_j)^2}{J}},$$

where J is the number of respondents. For the EVP battery this is:

```
sqrt(mean((theta_ests_real$EPV-complete_estimates)^2))
```

```
## [1] 0.6561699
```

To generalize this, we calculate the RMSE for the two adaptive item selection routines, a random inventory, the oracle battery, and the fixed inventory. In this case, the MEPV selection criteria slightly outperforms the MFI criteria but both significantly outperform the fixed and random batteries.

Table 3 RMSE for four-item selection options

Battery	RMSE
Fixed	0.814
MFI	0.664
MEPV	0.656
Random	0.863
Oracle	0.337

Using the oracle as a baseline, we see in Table 3 that the improvement of MEPV relative to the fixed battery is substantively meaningful, providing a $100\,((0.814 - 0.656)/0.337) = 46.29\%$ improvement in RMSE.

There is one important limitation to note about this exercise. We assumed in advance that the estimation method (e.g., MAP, EAP, or MLE) used for the complete response set was the "right" way to do it since this serves as our baseline. This makes it difficult or even impossible to compare estimation methods since they are essentially apples and oranges. That is, setting up a CAT that uses MAP estimates may not approximate EAP estimates, but this is not necessarily because one is more "correct."

5.2.2 Performance Based on Simulated Data

We can also compare models by simulating respondents. Here we will simulate 25 full response profiles for true values of $\theta = [-4, -3.5, ..., 3.5, 4]$. To do so, we use the simulateRespondents() function. This function takes a Cat object and the number of response profiles n to simulate given a value of θ_j.

We use the function adply() from the plyr package to conveniently repeat this procedure for different values of θ_j and store all results in a data frame.

```
poss_thetas <- seq(-4, 4, .5) # Values of theta we consider
set.seed(1)
respondents <- plyr::adply(.data = poss_thetas,
                    .margins = 1,
                    .id = NULL,
                    .fun = function(x){
                    simulateRespondents(catObj = nfc_cat,
                                    theta = x,
                                    n = 25)
                    })
```

The `respondents` data frame has 425 simulated response profiles (25 for each provided value of θ_j) and 18 columns (one column for each of the 18 NFC questions). Having multiple respondents for each value of θ_j helps take into account the probabilistic nature of the survey response. For a complete simulation study, researchers should consider more values of θ_j and more replicates per setting, as we do below.

We can use the `simulateThetas()` function with these simulated response profiles. In this case, `simulateThetas()` will administer two items adaptively to each respondent first using the EPV method, then again using the MFI method, and then again using random item selection. Estimates of the latent trait of each respondent using each method are returned as a data frame.

```
cat_list<-list(EPV=nfc_cat_EPV,
               MFI=nfc_cat_MFI,
               Random=nfc_cat_RANDOM) # CAT models to compare
sim_ests <- simulateThetas(catObjs = cat_list, responses = respondents)
colnames(sim_ests)<-c("EPV", "MFI", "Random")
```

We can also again calculate $\hat{\theta}_j$ estimates using the fixed and oracle methods.

```
# keep only columns for "fixed" battery
respondents_fixed <- respondents
respondents_fixed[,-which(colnames(respondents) %in% fixed_items)] <- NA

# generate fixed battery estimates
fixed_thetas <- estimateThetas(catObj = nfc_cat,
                               responses = respondents_fixed)

# now add new oracle estimates
# First make a vector of 25 respondents per theta value
true_thetas <- sort(rep(poss_thetas, 25))
# Now use the oracle battery
oracle_thetas <- oracle(catObj = nfc_cat,
                        theta = true_thetas,
                        responses = respondents)
```

Figure 22 visualizes the results by plotting the true value of θ on the x-axis, and the average absolute error $|\theta_j - \hat{\theta}|$ on the y-axis for different values of θ_j. First, notice that the oracle estimates of θ_j tend to be less accurate for more extreme positions on the latent trait. In other words, the question items in the battery work well for respondents toward the middle of the latent trait, but it

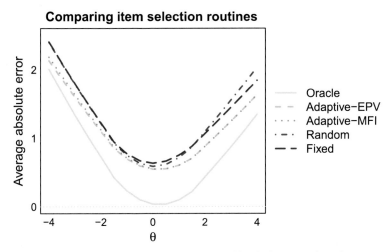

Figure 22 Simulation exercise to assess bias in latent trait estimates

is actually impossible to accurately estimate those with extreme positions by only asking two questions from this battery. This is actually a common result since question items tend to be written for moderate respondents.

Next, notice that $\hat{\theta}$s estimated from the fixed and random batteries do worse than the AIs in terms of absolute error across the entire range of θ_j. Thus, although adaptive methods perform similarly to each other, they both outperform the alternatives.

Finally, the *relative* improvement of the adaptive inventories is greatest for respondents farther from the center of the scale. We can think of the range of plausible values for the CAT batteries as being bounded by the random and oracle results. Toward the extremes, the adaptive battery covers nearly half of this ground, while toward the middle, all batteries perform similarly. This is again a very common result for AIs, reflecting the tendency for most items to be targeted toward the center of the distribution (where most respondents are located). It is the ability of AIs to administer the *right* question to the *right* respondents that offers the improved performance, and this is most visible for more unusual respondents.

5.2.3 Metrics for Model Evaluation and Test Information

In the discussion so far, we evaluated our proposed NFC adaptive battery in terms of RMSE and mean absolute error (MAE). However, it is important to note that these represent only two metrics for model evaluation. Others might include median absolute error, coverage probabilities, average posterior variance, or more. The simulation tools we provide combined with a little R coding will allow researchers to compare batteries using any or all of these metrics.

However, another diagnostic tool for evaluating an adaptive inventory is to examine how much Fisher information the battery gathers from respondents, or what we term *Fisher test information*. This relates to the final variance estimate of θ_j for each respondent, and it is also a widely used method of assessing batteries in the broader IRT literature.

We can again simulate having respondents go through a specific adaptive battery and record the resulting test information with the `simulateFisherInfo()` function. However, note that Fisher information must be calculated for some value of θ_j. This makes it especially attractive to evaluate the information using the true value of θ_j and a simulated response profile as we do here. In essence, we are calculating the Fisher test information for each battery taking into account the expected response patterns of respondents for different values of θ_j.

```
# Calculated Fisher information for simulated respondents
set.seed(1)
sim_fish <- simulateFisherInfo(catObjs = cat_list, theta = true_thetas,
                               responses = respondents)
colnames(sim_fish) <- c("EPV", "MFI", "Random")
```

We can also calculate the test information for the fixed inventory. This is not a built-in function, so we have to write a small loop.

```
# calculate test information for fixed battery
sim_fish$Fixed <- NA
for(i in 1:nrow(respondents_fixed)){
    nfc_cat@answers <- rep(NA, length(nfc_cat@answers))
    profile <- unlist(respondents_fixed[i, ])
    nfc_cat@answers[!is.na(profile)] <- profile[!is.na(profile)]
    sim_fish$Fixed[i] <- fisherTestInfo(nfc_cat, true_thetas[i])
}
```

If we wish, we could also include the oracle battery. This is less useful as a benchmark, however, because it chooses the battery that is most accurate, not the battery that maximizes information.

To assess model performance, we will plot these results relative to the baseline of random selection. This can be helpful because FI has no natural metric, and it is otherwise difficult to assess performance. That is, for each value of θ_j, we will calculate the average Fisher test information as $\overline{\mathbb{I}(\theta)}$ for the random,

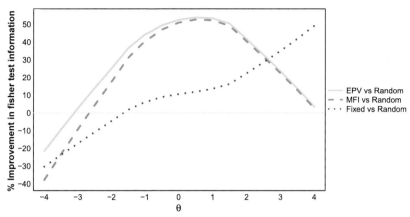

Figure 23 Average Fisher test information of adaptive test relative to a random baseline

fixed, and adaptive battery. We will then plot percentage improvement over the random battery. For instance, for the MFI battery we will calculate:

$$100 \times \frac{\overline{\mathbb{I}(\boldsymbol{\theta})}_{\text{MFI}} - \overline{\mathbb{I}(\boldsymbol{\theta})}_{\text{Random}}}{\overline{\mathbb{I}(\boldsymbol{\theta})}_{\text{Random}}}.$$

The results in Figure 23 show that MEPV performs modestly better than MFI, especially for low values of θ_j. Both also do surprisingly poorly for values of $\theta_j < -2.5$, suggesting that we may wish to explore alternative selection routines or priors **if** that area of the distribution is critical to our research question. Since very few respondents are located in that range in our empirical example, however, it is not a huge concern here. Further, both AIs do significantly better than the fixed battery except for at extremely high values of θ_j. This suggests that this fixed battery might be best calibrated for respondents in the highest region of the latent space.

5.3 Example: Assessing Batteries for Neuroticism

We conclude by reporting a more thorough validation of a single battery to provide a better example. Specifically, we examine a four-item adaptive measure of neuroticism from the "big five" factor model of personality (Costa and McCrae 2008). We want to create a reduced version of the 20-item neuroticism inventory. Each item consists of a statement (e.g., "I seldom feel blue.") and respondents evaluate each on a five-point scale ranging from '1' (Very inaccurate) to '5' (Very accurate). Note that this is the only example in this Element where not all of the raw data we use is available in the `catSurv` package.

We calibrated a GRM model using over 700,000 respondents collected by the myPersonality Project, a Facebook App that allowed participants to take personality inventories (Stillwell and Kosinski 2004). We also conducted a survey of 1,500 respondents with YouGov in June 2018 to create a representative sample. We use a normal prior distribution centered on the sample mean for the YouGov sample and a standard deviation of 1.2. This calibration is included in the `catSurv` package and additional details are available by running `?neuro_cat`.

Our aim is to evaluate alternative four-item CAT batteries. We will consider MLWI, PKL, EPV item selection routines. To assess the effects of the priors, we will also consider a model with the EPV criteria with a *t*-distribution prior with one degree of freedom. We will compare these with our standard baselines (oracle and random) as well as the four-item fixed neuroticism scale included in the 20-item Mini-IPIP (Donnellan et al. 2006).

We can set up all four CAT versions as well as our random battery.

```
data("neuro_cat") # load CAT object from package
setLengthThreshold(neuro_cat) <- 4 # All get same length threshold


# Replicate basic CAT model
neuro_cat_MLWI<-neuro_cat
neuro_cat_PKL<-neuro_cat
neuro_cat_EPV<-neuro_cat
neuro_cat_EPV_T1<-neuro_cat
neuro_cat_Random<-neuro_cat
```

We can now customize each battery to use different item selection routines, estimation methods, or priors.

```
setSelection(neuro_cat_MLWI)<-"MLWI"
setSelection(neuro_cat_PKL)<-"PKL"
setSelection(neuro_cat_EPV)<-"EPV"
setSelection(neuro_cat_EPV_T1)<-"EPV";
setPriorName(neuro_cat_EPV_T1)<-"STUDENT_T"
setPriorParams(neuro_cat_EPV_T1)<-c(-.025, 1) # Same center and 1 df
setSelection(neuro_cat_Random)<-"RANDOM"
```

5.3.1 Thinking about Diagnostics

In our evaluation, we will focus on three concerns. First, the batteries should be evaluated with the target population in mind. Different settings for CAT inventories will work better or worse depending on the distribution of the θ_j

parameters in the population we survey. A battery calibrated on a national sample, for instance, may be poorly suited for an evaluation in a clinical setting.

Second, we want to test the battery using a large number of response profiles (real and simulated) and look out for computational errors. Pay attention to warnings, and look out for instances when the entire battery is asked of a simulated respondent. Unusually bad estimates for specific respondents may also reflect numerical issues such as lack of convergence (e.g., for MLE θ estimation) or problems with the integration bounds (e.g., for MLWI item selection). In general, you want to find issues with your battery **before** you put it in the field. This is a particular concern since, for reasons of speed, catSurv is primarily a C++ program and errors are not always passed cleanly through to R. We have tried to insert checks to provide warnings, but in some cases the C++ error will simply crash R altogether. You do not want to be surprised in the field.

Third, always keep in mind that CAT is based on the assumption that the underlying IRT model is correct or at least good. The old adage "garbage in, garbage out" very much applies. If the item parameters are poorly estimated or if the measurement model itself is poorly structured, CAT can actually perform worse than a standard fixed battery. This is why it is useful to test your model using real response sets, particularly if they were not used to fit the original IRT parameters. Are the items loading well on the same underlying dimension? Are the item parameters the same (or similar) for the calibration sample and the target sample? If not, then CAT is probably not the right tool for the job.

5.3.2 Assessment in Practice

As a first step, we calculated estimates of θ_j for 3,000 random respondents using the standard defaults. We found that the range of the θ values was between -3.2 and 3.8 with most θ_j values heavily concentrated between -2 and 2. Preliminary testing showed that this battery experienced numerical problems that generated warnings for the MLWI item selection, which we solved by limiting the integration bounds.[8]

```
setUpperBound(neuro_cat_MLWI)<-4; setLowerBound(neuro_cat_MLWI)<- (-4)
setUpperBound(neuro_cat_PKL)<-4; setLowerBound(neuro_cat_PKL)<- (-4)
```

We then used the simulatedThetas function for each model separately for just the first 200 respondents and examined the output. We found no instances of extreme estimates or a lack of convergence. Assuming that our data is loaded into R as a data.frame called neuroData, we can then run our complete simulation study with one function.

---

[8] This can occur when P_{ijk} is estimated too close to 1 or 1.

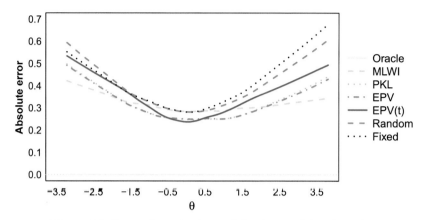

Figure 24 Comparing adaptive and fixed neuroticism batteries

```
cat_list<-list(MLWI=neuro_cat_MLWI,
               PKL=neuro_cat_PKL,
               EPV=neuro_cat_EPV,
               EPV_T1=neuro_cat_EPV_T1,
               Random=neuro_cat_Random)

cat_estimates<-simulateThetas(catObjs=cat_list, neuroData)
```

We can now assess the quality of these estimates relative to the $\hat{\theta}_j$ estimates we get when using respondents' answers to all 20 items.

We will also compare this to the performance of the fixed-reduced battery (Donnellan et al. 2006). Note this is not quite an apples-to-apples comparison because the wording for one item is modified.[9] In our view it is unlikely that this wording modification would affect the results here.

Table 4 shows that all of the AIs outperform both the fixed and random batteries. However, the PKL and MEPV batteries clearly outperform the MLWI and MEPV battery with a t-distribution prior. As expected, the oracle massively outperforms all others.

Figure 24 compares these scales across values of θ_j using simple LOWESS plots. The results show that PKL and MEPV perform almost identically across a range of θ_j values. The MEPV with t-distribution priors does well for individuals at the very center of the distribution, but worse everywhere else. Interestingly, the MLWI battery does slightly better than competitors for the most extreme respondents. However, there are very few respondents in these

---

[9] Our inventory has wording "I get stressed out easily" while the mini-IPIP says "I get upset easily."

Table 4 Model performance using real
respondent data

	RMSE	MAE
MLWI	0.452	0.346
PKL	0.391	0.302
MEPV	0.393	0.303
MEPV (*t* prior)	0.432	0.324
Random	0.489	0.376
Oracle	0.045	0.004
Fixed	0.478	0.365

regions leading to the overall results in Table 4. Finally, the fixed battery does uniformly worse than the AIs and even underperforms random selection for individuals where θ_j is large and positive.

Next, we will create a set of *simulated* response profiles for different values of θ_j in Figure 25. We use the `simulateRespondents()` function to create 100 complete response profiles for a sequence of θ values ranging from -3 to 3.5 at intervals of 0.1. This results in 6,700 complete response profiles. We chose this range based on our empirical results mentioned at the beginning of Section 5.3.2. If you are investigating a population that is more unusual, you will want to concentrate the θ_j values in a more targeted interval.

For each respondent, we simulate walking them through each of the four-item inventories and then record their final θ_j estimate as well as their estimated test information. This can all be done with `simulateRespondents()`, `simulateThetas()`, and `simulateFisherInfo()`. Here we plot absolute error and test information across values of θ focusing on the raw output (rather than relative to the random baseline). We see that all of the AIs again do uniformly better than the fixed and random batteries. Assuming that we are targeting a population similar to our empirical sample, this evidence again suggests we can stick with the default MEPV battery. If we anticipate giving a survey to a more extreme population, MLWI may still not be the best approach since we could also re-center the prior distribution.

5.4 Summary

The tools in this section are designed to help researchers evaluate the quality of their adaptive inventory. Given a calibrated model, we can assess which (if any) CAT options will work to improve our final measures. We discussed comparing models in terms of speed, accuracy, and information using real and simulated

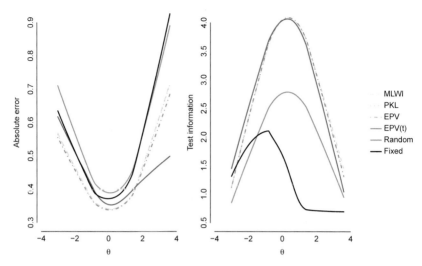

Figure 25 Comparing adaptive and fixed neuroticism batteries

data. We also introduced the concept of using oracle and random models as baselines to facilitate meaningful comparison. Throughout, we highlighted the importance of thinking carefully about the target population when assessing any particular model.

6 Tools and Tricks for Applied Researchers

The previous sections of this Element provide a theoretical overview of adaptive inventories alongside an introduction to the functionality of the `catSurv` R package. But there are still practical problems with fielding an AI we have not discussed. This final section provides guidance as well as some tools and tricks we've developed to smooth this process.

Once again, however, there is no way we can provide universal advice. Before we start, therefore, we encourage interested readers to join the discussion group located at `https://groups.google.com/g/catsurv`. This is a forum where you can ask questions or pass on your own tricks and ideas on how to integrate adaptive surveys into the survey process.

In this section, we focus on two concerns. First, in order to use CAT, researchers need a calibrated inventory. Earlier sections showed how to do that mechanically given the right data, but what goes into this data-collection process? Second, once we have calibrated a model and run diagnostics, how do we get the survey into the field? We address these issues in turn.

6.1 Building a Battery

The first problem is finding data for the *entire* battery needed for calibration. The easiest solution to this problem is to use an adaptive battery based on existing data. For example, the `catSurv` package includes pre-calibrated batteries for:

- the big five personality inventory,
- need for affect,
- need to evaluate,
- need for cognition,
- systematizing quotient,
- empathy quotient,
- right-wing authoritarianism,
- social dominance orientation, and
- the Schwartz values index.

We fit these models on large samples of at least 6,000 respondents, including at least one nationally representative sample. These models are included as `Cat` objects in the `catSurv` package, and their associated help files include information about the original samples. Go use them! Researchers with their own calibration data sets are encouraged to help us expand this list. Researchers with their own calibrated adaptive batteries are invited to contribute them to the `catSurv` package `https://github.com/erossiter/catSurv`.

Researchers may want to field an adaptive version of an inventory we have not provided, which means you will need your own sample. Two primary concerns arise when collecting these data. First, how big should the sample size be? And second, how "representative" does the sample need to be?

6.1.1 How Big?

We conducted a simulation to investigate the effect of sample size on the estimation of item parameters. We use the neuroticism data detailed in Section 5.3. We use this data for our simulation because nearly one million participants took the 20-item battery, allowing us to get a sense of what optimal item parameters should be by looking at the full sample and comparing results to smaller calibration sample sizes.

Specifically, using the 20 item neuroticism scale, we assumed a sample size of $n \in [100, 1000, 2000, 500010000, 100000]$, drew 10 samples of respondents per sample size, and estimated item parameters with each randomly drawn sample of respondents using the `grmCat()` function.

Figure 26 plots the results of this exericse for 9 randomly selected items' discrimination parameters. The gray line indicates the discrimination parameter estimated using complete cases in the full sample (n = 774,410). The variation in the parameter estimates shrinks considerably toward the gray line as the sample size increases, meaning the parameter estimates become

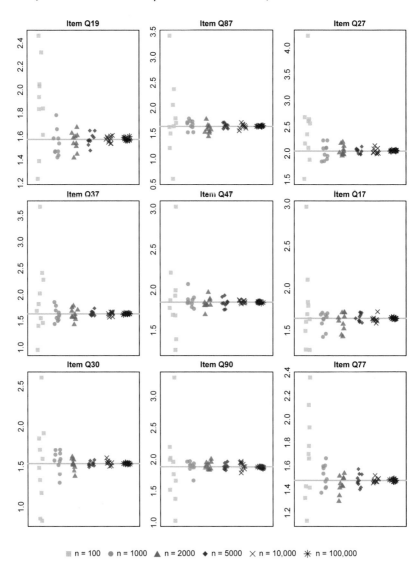

 n = 100 ● n = 1000 ▲ n = 2000 ◆ n = 5000 ✕ n = 10,000 ✳ n = 100,000

Figure 26 Simulation varying calibration sample sizes for neuroticism scale. GRM discrimination parameters for neuroticism estimated using 10 random samples for increasingly larger sample sizes. Gray line indicates parameter estimates using the full sample (n = 774,410).

increasingly similar to the full sample estimates. For this inventory, we think the calibration size ought to be at least 2,000. This conclusion depends on inventory-specific features such as the number of questions in the battery. However, our general advice is that batteries should be calibrated with *at least* 1,000 respondents and preferably several thousand. Researchers should also pay special attention to items with very few respondents choosing specific response categories. In these cases, the category-specific parameters can be unstable. If this happens, researchers might consider collapsing adjacent categories or ensuring that this item category is not chosen frequently during diagnostics and pretesting.

6.1.2 Calibration Samples and Choosing a Prior

To calibrate the adaptive inventory, it is important to have a *large* sample of *diverse* respondents (meaning there is a lot of variation on the latent trait). As Embretson (1996) notes, "Unbiased estimates of item properties may be obtained from unrepresentative samples" (p. 342). What is needed to calibrate CAT models is not so much a representative sample, as a sample that is large and diverse along the dimension of interest.

However, it *is* important to select a prior to reflect our belief about distribution of the latent trait in our target population. In general, we want to choose priors that reflect the plausible distribution of values for the latent trait in the population we are studying.

As an example, we will continue to use the neuroticism battery. In addition to the large, diverse sample collected by the myPersonality Project discussed in Section 5, we also collected a nationally representative sample through YouGov. We first fit a model using 5,000 respondents from the large, diverse sample and then the representative YouGov sample. We then estimated respondents' positions on the latent trait using a pooled model.

Next, we chose a prior reflecting the true *national* distribution of the neuroticism trait. Assuming we plan to administer the battery to a national sample, we used the YouGov sample as our benchmark. The thick orange line in Figure 27 shows the selected prior, which is a normal prior centered at the mean of the YouGov estimates and a standard deviation of 1.2. This figure also shows the distribution of neuroticism estimates for the two samples as well as the distribution when pooling the samples together. We see that the selected prior adequately encapsulates the values of the latent trait estimates in both samples.

6.2 Getting to the Field

Once the battery has been calibrated and tested, the final step is to put it in the field. This is, perhaps, the most challenging step in that no one can provide universal software or advice. Nonetheless, here we discuss two approaches for integrating adaptive batteries into real world surveys. First, we discuss precalculating branching schemes. In Section 6.3 we then discuss interacting with the `https://catsurv.com` webservice.

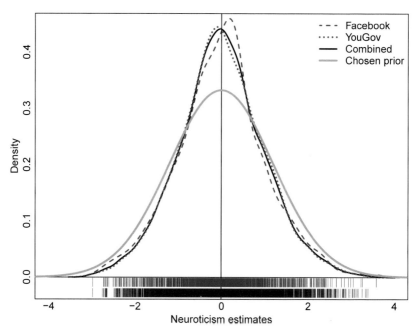

Figure 27 Densities of neuroticism estimates for the YouGov, myPersonality, and pooled samples. The figure shows the density for the estimated ability parameters for two separate samples as well as the pooled sample. The rugs indicate respondents' estimated locations on the underlying latent scale. We then build an AI using the prior density (shown as the thick orange line), which is centered at the mean position of the YouGov sample with standard deviation chosen to encapsulate the values of the latent trait estimates in both samples.

In many settings, the most practical approach to administering an adaptive inventory may be to precalculate a complete branching scheme or "tree." A branching scheme is useful because it enumerates all possible adaptive inventories that may arise when administering the survey. The `catSurv` packages includes functionality to make this as easy as possible. Note, however, this tree of all possible response profiles can easily become very complex, with the number of response profiles equal to C^{n-1}, where C is the number of possible response options and n is the number of questions that will be administered. However, since short batteries are more of a rule than an exception in survey settings, this might be the best way to go if you can get your survey firm to cooperate.

To demonstrate the use of a precalculated branching scheme, we will walk through the 2016 ANES Pilot Study's administration of an adaptive need to evaluate (NTE) inventory. (See Montgomery and Rossiter (2020) for a similar example of fielding the need for cognition adaptive battery (Cacioppo and

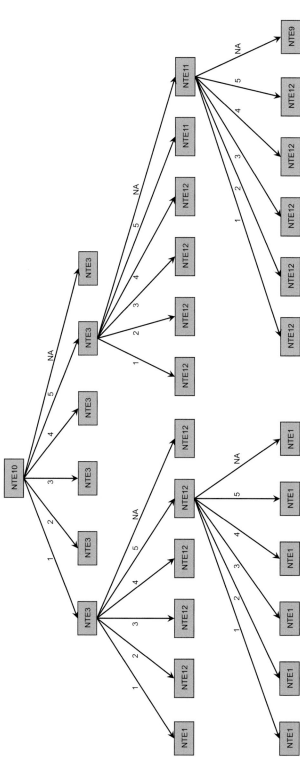

Figure 28 Portions of a complete branching scheme for the four-item need to evaluate adaptive inventory. The figure describes selected sub-trees of the complete branching scheme for the four-item need to evaluate adaptive inventory included on the 2016 ANES Pilot Study. The labels on the branches indicate possible respondent answers. An "NA" indicates item nonresponse.

Petty 1982).) This battery was introduced by Jarvis and Petty (1996) as "a measure designed to assess individual differences in the propensity to engage in evaluation" (p. 172).

Since this battery has six response options (a five-item Likert scale and nonresponse), and the stopping rule is to administer four items, the tree contains only $6^3 = 216$ complete branchings, and the entire tree can be represented as a table with 259 rows. We provided the table to YouGov in advance, and the survey was administered to 1,200 respondents drawn from an opt-in online panel. Figure 28 depicts portions of the scheme for the four-item NTE adaptive inventory. The labels on the branches indicate possible answers. (The NA indicates item nonresponse.) For example, a respondent who answers '1' to NTE3 will be asked NTE1, and a respondent who then answers '5' will be asked NTE12.

To calibrate the adaptive personality inventory, we combined data from three samples (more information available in the help file: ?nte).

```
data(nte)
nte_cat_anes <- grmCat(nte)
```

Given some stopping rule, the function makeTree() will determine all potential branches of questions that the respondents might traverse. The ANES Pilot Study had room for only four questions, thus before using the makeTree() function, we specify this stopping rule in the Cat object. Note the estimation routine, item selection routine, and any other researcher-specified option for the CAT algorithm should be set before calling the makeTree() function, just as these options should be specified before using an adaptive inventory in real time.

```
setLengthThreshold(nte_cat_anes) <- 4
setPriorName(nte_cat_anes) <- "NORMAL"
setPriorParams(nte_cat_anes) <- c(0, 1.2)
setEstimation(nte_cat_anes) <- "EAP"
```

The makeTree() function has two options for the format of the output indicated by the argument flat. If flat = TRUE, then the tree will be in the format of a complete look-up table. If flat = FALSE, then the tree will be a list of lists representing the branching schemes given a provided response profile. We recommend using the flattened tree for a more intuitive representation in the form of a look-up table. However, the "list of lists" approach is a more efficient way to store the battery and will allow for faster look-up speeds.

```
nte_table <- makeTree(nte_cat_anes, flat = TRUE)
```

The table's columns represent the battery items and the rows represent the possible answer profiles. Thus, there is a column for every question item as well as a final column indicating the "next item" to ask given the row's answer profile. The first row of the table shows no questions have been administered (all are NA), therefore the first question to ask all respondents is q10.

```
nte_table[1,]
```

##	q1	q2	q3	q4	q5	q6
##	NA	NA	NA	NA	NA	NA
##	q7	q8	q9	q10	q11	q12
##	NA	NA	NA	NA	NA	NA
##	q13	q14	q15	q16	NextItem	
##	NA	NA	NA	NA	"q10"	

Using the look-up table then proceeds as follows. Find the row in which column q10 indicates the respondent's answer. If the respondent answered option '1' to q10, the row in the look-up table that shows that response profile then indicates which item to ask next. Note that the makeTree() function considers nonresponse (indicated by a −1 in the look-up table) to count against the stopping rule, such that the survey would end if a respondent refused to answer their first four questions.

6.3 Interfacing with Webservice and Qualtrics

While a tree or look-up table might be preferable for some survey firms, for larger inventories it can become unwieldy and even slow. Moreover, researches conducting their own survey may be unable to create custom programming to make use of the table. To address this issue, we created https://catsurv.com. This is a webservice based on the OpenCPU system that essentially hosts a stable and quick version of the catSurv package (Ooms 2014). The OpenCPU framework in principle allows for any survey software to interact with catSurv, and web developers should be able to fully integrate our software into their operations.

But most researchers are not web developers. Therefore, we provide a detailed explanation for how to integrate AIs into the popular Qualtrics survey software at https://catsurv.com. We have successfully used Qualtrics to interact with catSurv to administer AIs in several of our own research projects. However, it can take some trial and error to get it set up correctly, so be sure to pretest and bring issues to our Google group: https://groups.google.com/g/catsurv.

7 Implications and Future Directions

Survey researchers face trade-offs. On the one hand, they want to accurately measure latent concepts of interest, something that often leads to long batteries. On the other hand, they need to keep surveys short because in the world of survey research, time is literally money. In the end, this tension cannot be eliminated. However, we believe that adaptive batteries offer a partial solution by allowing researchers to make the most of their survey space and to get the best possible estimates of the latent traits they care about.

Adaptive surveys offer a method for achieving superior measurement relative to fixed batteries of the same length. Despite their promise, further improvements are possible. In particular, survey researchers face several data quality challenges including: (a) strict limits on battery length, (b) relatively high levels of measurement error, and (c) concerns about the stability of item calibrations. Further research as to how these issues can be addressed within the CAT framework is clearly warranted.

One promising extension would be to allow the batteries to "start" from a better place. Including informative priors in the CAT algorithm could tackle this issue. For instance, we might assume that individuals who say they pay close attention to politics might on average have higher latent positions on political knowledge. What is the best way to include this prior information into the algorithm that will lead to superior estimates?

Relatedly, it seems reasonable that scores on individual latent traits are not necessarily independent. For multidimensional scales, it may be possible to adapt the entire battery so that each question improves item selection across *multiple* latent dimension (Segall 1996). These kinds of approaches may make CAT even more efficient for estimating latent traits with as few question items as possible.

Moreover, survey respondents can be inattentive and responses may have high levels of error. This is particularly worrisome because "wrong" answers early in the battery can lead to inefficiencies and even bias when these mistakes are further propagated and reinforced by the CAT algorithm. The CAT batteries may benefit from methods designed to prevent over-fitting estimates in the early stages of the algorithm (e.g., Chang and Ying 1999; Chen, Ankenmann, and Chang 2000).

Finally, researchers may be concerned that item parameters are unstable across administrations of the survey or between distinct subgroups. Items on a political knowledge battery, for example, might fluctuate over time in regard to how they relate to latent political knowledge. This can negatively affect the accuracy of final estimates. Further extensions of the approach outlined here could take into account "differential item functioning," wherein the algorithm could actively search for instances where items are not behaving as intended within new samples or within specific subsamples (Wang, Tay, and Drasgow 2013).

We will close by noting that adaptive batteries invite a different approach to survey battery development. In many cases, researchers developing batteries avoid "extreme" items because they can be informative for only a subset of respondents. With CAT it is possible – and even desirable – to set aside these concerns and try to develop survey items that are calibrated for individuals at all values of the latent trait. Adaptive batteries will then be better able to select the best items for all respondents. Developing inventories that take CAT into account could dramatically improve the quality of measurement for more "extreme" individuals in survey research without reducing the measurement quality for more average respondents.

References

Altemeyer, Bob. 1988. *Enemies of freedom: Understanding right-wing authoritarianism*. San Fransisco, CA: Jossey-Bass.

Ames, Daniel R., Paul Rose, and Cameron P. Anderson. 2006. "The NPI-16 as a short measure of narcissism." *Journal of Research in Personality* 40(4): 440–450.

Baker, Frank B., and Seock-Ho Kim. 2004. *Item response theory: Parameter estimation techniques*. New York: Marcel Dekker.

Bakker, Bert N., and Yphtach Lelkes. 2018. "Selling ourselves short? How abbreviated measures of personality change the way we think about personality and politics." *The Journal of Politics* 80(4): 1311–1325.

Berinsky, Adam J., Michele F. Margolis, Michael W. Sances, and Christopher Warshaw. 2019. "Using screeners to measure respondent attention on self-administered surveys: Which items and how many?" *Political Science Research and Methods*, 9(2), 430–437.

Birnbaum, Allan. 1968. "Some latent train models and their use in inferring an examinee's ability." In F. M. Lord and M. R. Novick (eds.), *Statistical theories of mental test scores* (395–479). Reading, MA: Addison-Wesley.

Bizer, George Y. Jon A. Krosnick, Richard E. Petty, Derek D. Rucker, and S. Christian Wheeler. 2000. National Election Studies Report. "Need for cognition and need to evaluate in the 1998 national election survey pilot study."

Cacioppo, John T., and Richard E. Petty. 1982. "The need for cognition." *Journal of Personality & Social Psychology* 42(1): 116–131.

Chang, Hua-Hua, and Zhiliang Ying. 1996. "A global information approach to computerized adaptive testing." *Applied Psychological Measurement* 20(3): 213–229.

Chang, Hua-Hua, and Zhiliang Ying. 1999. "A-stratified multistage computerized adaptive testing." *Applied Psychological Measurement* 23(3): 211–222.

Chen, Shu-Ying, Robert D. Ankenmann, and Hua-Hua Chang. 2000. "A comparison of item selection rules at the early stages of computerized adaptive testing." *Applied Psychological Measurement* 24(3): 241–255.

Choi, Seung W., and Richard J. Swartz. 2009. "Comparison of CAT item selection criteria for polytomous items." *Applied Psychological Measurement* 33(6): 419–440.

Costa, Paul T., and Robert R. McCrae. 2008. "The revised neo personality inventory (neo-pi-r)." In G. J. Boyle, G. Matthews, and D. H. Saklofske (eds.), *The SAGE handbook of personality theory and assessment, Vol. 2. Personality measurement and testing* (179–198). SAGE Publications.

Delli Carpini, Michael X., and Scott Keeter. 1993. "Measuring political knowledge: Putting first things first." *American Journal of Political Science* 37(4): 1179–1206.

Delli Carpini, Michael X., and Scott Keeter. 1996. *What Americans know about politics and why it matters*. New Haven, CT: Yale University Press.

Dodd, Barbara G., R. J. De Ayala, and William R. Koch. 1995. "Computerized adaptive testing with polytomous items." *Applied Psychological Measurement* 19(1): 5–22.

Donnellan, M. Brent, Oswald, Frederick L. Baird, Brendan M. Lucas, Richard E. 2006. "The mini-IPIP scales: Tiny-yet-effective measures of the big five factors of personality." *Psychological Assessment* 18(2): 192–203.

Druckman, James N. 2004. "Political preference formation: Competition, deliberation, and the (ir)relevance of framing effects." *American Political Science Review* 98(4): 671–686.

Embretson, Susan E. 1996. "The new rules of measurement." *Psychological Assessment* 8(4): 341–349.

Enamorado, Ted. 2018. "Active learning for probabilistic record linkage." Social Science Research Network (SSRN). URL: https://ssrn.com/abstract53257638.

Groves, Robert M., and Steven G. Heeringa. 2006. "Responsive design for household surveys: Tools for actively controlling survey errors and costs." *Journal of the Royal Statistical Society: Series A (Statistics in Society)* 169(3): 439–457.

Herzog, A. Regula, and Jerald G. Bachman. 1981. "Effects of questionnaire length on response quality." *Public Opinion Quarterly* 45(4): 549–559.

Hetherington, Marc J., and Jonathan D. Weiler. 2009. *Authoritarianism and polarization in American politics*. Cambridge: Cambridge University Press.

Hetherington, Marc, and Elizabeth Suhay. 2011. "Authoritarianism, threat, and Americans' support for the War on Terror." *American Journal of Political Science* 55(3): 546–560.

Jarvis, W. Blair G., and Richard E. Petty. 1996. "The need to evaluate." *Journal of Personality and Social Psychology* 70(1): 172–194.

Kaufman, Aaron R. 2020. "Implementing novel, flexible, and powerful survey designs in r shiny." *PloS one* 15(4): e0232424.

Kingsbury, G. Gage, and David J. Weiss. 1983. "A comparison of IRT-based adaptive mastery testing and a sequential mastery testing procedure."

In David J. Weiss, (ed.), *New horizons in testing: Latent trait test theory and computerized adaptive testing*, (257–283). New York: Academic Press.

Miller, Blake, Fridolin Linder, and Walter R. Mebane. 2019. "Active learning approaches for labeling text: Review and assessment of the performance of active learning approaches." *Political Analysis* 28(4), 532–551.

Montgomery, Jacob M., and Josh Cutler. 2013. "Computerized adaptive testing for public opinion surveys." *Political Analysis* 21(2): 172–192.

Montgomery, Jacob M., and Erin L. Rossiter. 2017. "CatSurv: Computerized adaptive testing for survey research." `https://CRAN.R-project.org/package=catSurv`.

Montgomery, Jacob M., and Erin L. Rossiter. 2020. "So many questions, so little time: Integrating adaptive inventories into public opinion research." *Journal of Survey Statistics and Methodology*, 8(4), 667–690.

Moore, Ryan T., and Sally A. Moore. 2013. "Blocking for sequential political experiments." *Political Analysis* 21(4): 507.

Muraki, Eiji. 1992. "A generalized partial credit model: Application of an em algorithm." *ETS Research Report Series* 1992(1): i–30.

Muraki, Eiji, and Mari Muraki. 2016. "Generalized partial credit model." In Wim J. van der Linden (ed.), *Handbook of item response theory*, vol.1 (155–166). Boca Raton, FL: Chapman & Hall/CRC, p. 155–166.

Offer-Westort, Molly, Alexander Coppock, and Donald P. Green. 2021. "Adaptive experimental design: Prospects and applications in political science." *American Journal of Political Science* 65(4): 826–844.

Ooms, Jeroen. 2014. "The OpenCPU system: Towards a universal interface for scientific computing through separation of concerns." https://arxiv.org/pdf/1406.4806.pdf.

Pawitan, Yudi. 2001. *In all likelihood: Statistical modelling and inference using likelihood*. Oxford: Oxford University Press.

Raskin, Robert, and Howard Terry. 1988. "A principal-components analysis of the narcissistic personality inventory and further evidence of its construct validity." *Journal of Personality and Social Psychology* 54(5): 890–902.

Rizopoulos, Dimitris. 2006. "Ltm: An rR package for latent variable modeling and item response theory analyses." *Journal of Statistical Software* 17(5): 1–25.

Salganik, Matthew J., and Karen E. C. Levy. 2015. "Wiki surveys: Open and quantifiable social data collection." *PloS one* 10(5): e0123483.

Samejima, Fumiko. 1969. "Estimation of latent ability using a response pattern of graded scores." *Psychometrika Monograph Supplement* 34(4): 100, Number 17.

Schwartz, Shalom H. 1992. "Universals in the content and structure of values: Theoretical advances and empirical tests in 20 countries." In Mark P. Zanna (ed.), *Advances in experimental social psychology*, vol. 25 (1–65). New York: Academic Press.

Segall, Daniel O. 1996. "Multidimensional adaptive testing." *Psychometrika* 61(2): 331–354.

Segall, Daniel O. 2005. "Computerized adaptive testing." In Kimberly Kempf-Leonard (ed.), *Encylopedia of social measurement*, (429–438). Oxford: Elsevier.

Sheatsley, Paul B. 1983. "Questionnaire construction and item writing." In P. H. Rossi, J. D. Wright, and A. B. Anderson (eds.), *Handbook of survey research* (195–230). San Diego, CA: Academic Press.

Sidanius, Jim Felicia Pratto, Colette Van Laar, Shana Levin. 2004. "Social dominance theory: Its agenda and method." *Political Psychology* 25(6): 845–880.

Stillwell, David J., and Michal Kosinski. 2004. "MyPersonality project: Example of successful utilization of online social networks for large-scale social research." *American Psychologist* 59(2): 93–104.

van der Linden, Wim J. 1998. "Bayesian item selection criteria for adaptive testing." *Psychometrika* 63(2): 201–216.

van der Linden, Wim J., and Peter J. Pashley. 2010. *Elements of adaptive testing*. New York: Springer.

Velez, Yamil Ricardo, and Howard Lavine. 2017. "Racial diversity and the dynamics of authoritarianism." *The Journal of Politics* 79(2): 519–533.

Wang, Wei, Louis Tay, and Fritz Drasgow. 2013. "Detecting differential item functioning of polytomous items for an ideal point response process." *Applied Psychological Measurement* 37(4): 316–335.

Warm, Thomas A. 1989. "Weighted likelihood estimation of ability in item response theory." *Psychometrika* 54(3): 427–450.

Weiss, David J. 1982. "Improving measurement quality and efficiency with adaptive testing." *Applied Psychological Measurement* 6(4): 473–492.

Weiss, David J., and G. Gage Kingsbury. 1984. "Application of computerized adaptive testing to educational problems." *Journal of Educational Measurement* 21(4): 361–375.

Acknowledgments

We are grateful to Josh Cutler, Tom Wilkinson, Haley Acevedo, Alex Weil, Ryden Butler, Matt Malis, Joshua Landman, and Min Hee Seo for their programming assistance. Valuable feedback for this project was provided by Harold Clarke, Brendan Nyhan, and audience members at Washington University in St. Louis, the University of Chicago, Dartmouth College, New York University, and Princeton University. Funding for this project was provided by the Weidenbaum Center on the Economy, Government, and Public Policy and the National Science Foundation (SES-1558907).

Data Availability Statement

The replication files accompanying this Element can be run interactively online via Code Ocean. The link can be found below:

https://doi.org/10.24433/CO.3138309.v2

Cambridge Elements ☰

Quantitative and Computational Methods for the Social Sciences

R. Michael Alvarez
California Institute of Technology

R. Michael Alvarez has taught at the California Institute of Technology his entire career, focusing on elections, voting behavior, election technology, and research methodologies. He has written or edited a number of books (recently, *Computational Social Science: Discovery and Prediction* and *Evaluating Elections: A Handbook of Methods and Standards*) and numerous academic articles and reports.

Nathaniel Beck
New York University

Nathaniel Beck is Professor of Politics at NYU (and Affiliated Faculty at the NYU Center for Data Science) where he has been since 2003, before which he was Professor of Political Science at the University of California, San Diego. He is the founding editor of the quarterly, *Political Analysis*. He is a fellow of both the American Academy of Arts and Sciences and the Society for Political Methodology.

About the Series
The Elements Series Quantitative and Computational Methods for the Social Sciences contains short introductions and hands-on tutorials to innovative methodologies. These are often so new that they have no textbook treatment or no detailed treatment on how the method is used in practice. Among emerging areas of interest for social scientists, the series presents machine learning methods, the use of new technologies for the collection of data, and new techniques for assessing causality with experimental and quasi-experimental data.

Cambridge Elements ≡

Quantitative and Computational Methods for the Social Sciences

Printed in the United States
by Baker & Taylor Publisher Services